The Family Idea Book:
Praying and Playing Together

The Family Idea Book:

Praying and Playing Together

by

Matilda Nordtvedt

MOODY PRESS
CHICAGO

Library of Congress Cataloging in Publication Data

Nordtvedt, Matilda.
  The family idea book.

  Bibliography: p.
  1. Family—Religious life. I. Title.
BV4526.2.N67 1984   249   84-16655
ISBN: 0-8024-0436-7 (pbk.)

1 2 3 4 5 6 7 Printing BC Year 88 87 86 85 84

Printed in the United States of America

Contents

Introduction

The family is in trouble. Homes are breaking up at an alarming rate. Even in homes where family members stay together, there is little real "togetherness." In one large American city a survey showed that fewer than half of its families ate together three times a week!

Sixty-one percent of the people polled by the White House Conference on Families admitted that their family was the most important part of their lives. Over half of those polled agreed that family life has indeed deteriorated.

An acquaintance of ours decided that the only way to preserve his family was to take them out into the wilds of Oregon, far away from the pressures and complexities and conveniences of modern life. The children study at home by correspondence. In the evenings, instead of rushing off to the PTA, a prayer meeting, or a basketball game, the family sits in front of a cozy fire cracking nuts, reading, and enjoying one another's company.

Although we may envy this family, few of us would want to isolate ourselves and our children to this extent. We must stay in the mainstream of society. But how can we cope?

Our children face pressures we never even dreamed of a generation ago. A high school girl recently told her mother that she avoids using the restroom at school all day because it is constantly filled with girls smoking marijuana. At another school in our city some children (even seventh graders) come to school drunk. These problems have become so widespread that in many cases the authorities have given up trying to control them. The same is true of runaway children; there are too many today for police departments to track them down adequately.

Parents too are under more pressure than ever before. Inflation demands longer working hours with both parents working in many cases. Stay-at-home mothers are made to feel inferior by advocates of women's rights. The affluency and materialism of our society tempt us to accept a distorted value system. Our homes are bombarded with the perverted views of the world through television and other media.

The home is under attack, and many families are crumbling. There is only one power strong enough to prevent this from happening to your home—God's power. The means He has given you is His Word.

If we lived out in the wilderness and spent our evenings cracking nuts before the fire, we would have no problem finding time to teach God's Word to our children. But we don't live in the wilderness; we live in a bustling community with all kinds of pressures and demands not only for our time and attention, but also for that of our children. As we all go in different directions, how can we have family devotions? If we seldom even eat together, how can we find opportunity to pray together?

As we need physical food every day, we also need spiritual food. We wouldn't think of depriving our children of a nutritious breakfast, lunch, and dinner. But how often does our family go for days without spiritual nourishment?

The ideal is to have family devotions every day. For some families this is almost impossible. I remember how difficult that was even twenty years ago when we were rearing our family. Today, as life has become increasingly hectic, it is even harder.

What shall we do? Throw up our hands and give up? That's what Satan would have us do. Instead, look at it this way: If you can't manage family devotions every day, have them every other day. If that seems impossible, determine to have them once a week. God will help you work out a time suitable for everyone if you are really in earnest. Francis Schaeffer has written in his book *True Spirituality,* "On this side of the fall and before Christ comes, we must not insist on 'perfection or nothing' or we will end with the 'nothing' " (p. 136). That goes for family devotions, too.

God told Israel through Moses: "And these words, which I am commanding you today, shall be on your heart; and you shall teach them diligently to your sons and shall talk of them when you sit in your house and when you walk by the way and when you lie down and when you rise up" (Deuteronomy 6:6-7). In other words, incorporate God's Word into your life, bringing God's principles into everyday situations. Teach your children to look at life from God's point of view whether it's concerning a sick kitten, a lost girlfriend, or a decision between colleges.

What About Play?   Play is not a luxury in our day—it is a necessity. We are uptight much of the time and must learn to relax. We need to lay aside our work and enjoy our families. Recreation is what it says— re-creation. We are revitalized when we play.

We were invited to a family party one night recently, but I was so tired after working all day I didn't relish the thought of going. When I got there, however, my weariness vanished as I engaged in interesting games and pleasant conversation. I came home relaxed as well as stimulated. Play has been called a companion to work because of its rejuvenating powers.

Too often Mom and Dad either do not find time to play or play with others rather than with their children. It's important to *pray* together as a family, but it is also important to *play* together.

Perhaps it is impossible for you to spend time every day entering into your children's activities. My husband, a pastor, couldn't. Nearly every evening he had to rush off to a meeting. We tried, however, to set aside Friday evenings for Family Night when we could do things at home together. Our boys looked forward to that night, because they could have Dad all to themselves!

Family Night can be a teaching time as well as a fun time, a time to draw the family closer together and closer to God. This book aims to help you establish a Family Night in your home. It is the product of hindsight, mistakes, victories, and insights gained from the Word of God. I hope its suggestions will be a help in keeping your family intact in our crumbling society.

What About Age Differences?   It is comparatively easy to have family devotions and family fun times if your children are in the same age bracket. Our oldest was three-and-a-half when our third child was born, so we never had the problem of teenagers and toddlers in the same family. Many do, however. How can you handle this? If you aim at the teenagers, the toddlers become restless. If you aim at the toddlers, the teenagers are bored. Even junior age children resent "baby stuff."

One way to get around this is to enlist the help of your older children to teach the younger ones. This can be done in a variety of ways. How about making scrapbooks for your toddlers with pictures to illustrate simple Bible verses? Older chldren can search through magazines for pictures, draw pictures, or even take pictures with a camera to illustrate the verses.

Helping teach younger brothers and sisters will give older children a sense of responsibility for the little ones in the family (as well as reinforce scriptural truth in their own lives). Of course care must be taken to concentrate on the older children as well.

The suggested devotions in this book can be simplified for younger children. This is true also of many of the family activities. Perhaps what is presented here will spark your creativity, and you will come up with some good ideas of your own.

Some teenagers will not be interested in teaching younger brothers and sisters. They may not be interested in family devotions at all. One mother I know, in desperation, stood in the hallway and read the Bible to her husband and sons who had retreated to their rooms and shut the doors.

We must expect some opposition to our efforts to make God's life-changing Word a part of our families. Don't be discouraged—be flexible. If one method doesn't work, try another. If you can't do everything, do something. Stay cheerful and in fellowship with God yourself no matter how difficult it may become. Above all, pray for your family. "The effective prayer of a righteous man can accomplish much" (James 5:16).

1
January

The early Christians refused to call the first month of the year "January," because it was named after the Roman god Janus. The Romans believed that Janus, a deity with two faces, could not only look in two directions at once but also knew the past as well as the future. He was honored as the god of the door or gate and the god of beginnings.

Julius Caesar decided when he invented the twelve-month calendar to give the first month of the year the name of that all-knowing, all-seeing god. Janus was honored during the entire month of January as the priests burned fire on twelve altars representing the twelve months of the year.

The early Christians, not wanting to have anything to do with a pagan religion, called the first month of the year First Month and did not celebrate their new year until March 25. The Christian new year was not changed to January 1 in Europe until 1582, and not in England until 1752. Today we call our first month January with no thought of its original meaning.

Janus or no Janus, we do look both backward and forward as we begin a new year. We look back to the year that has passed to rejoice over victories won and blessings received and to repent of failures and mistakes. We look forward to the coming year with anticipation. How can we make it better than the year that has just passed? How can we be more successful in our endeavors?

The new year is an untried path. We have not walked this way before, but God has not left us without a guidebook for the road before us. He has given us His Word. Its principles will guide us, its promises encourage us, its precepts teach us. He says to us and our families at the beginning of this new year, "For I know the plans that I have for you...plans for welfare and not for calamity to give you a future and a hope" (Jeremiah 29:11).

You can enter the new year confidently with your hand in His!

ESPECIALLY FOR PARENTS

Our government has so many records it would take two thousand years to destroy them at the rate of one per minute. However, the advent of the computer and the possibility of keeping records on easy-to-store microfilm should alleviate some of the storage problems.

The abundance of government records may sometimes seem to be unnecessary "red tape," but record keeping is important. What better time to begin keeping systematic family records than at the beginning of a new year?

Medical Records

Remember all those questions the nurse asks you at the doctor's office? It's hard to know the answers unless you've written the facts down. Doctors' medical records can be lost in transit from one place to another. How important it is for you to keep your own.

In order to help you and your family, doctors need to know specific details. Vague guesses are not of much value. Accurate information regarding past diseases of family members, allergies, immunizations, and injuries is essential in order that a doctor may do his best.

Tetanus shots are believed to be effective for ten years. How many of us have subjected a family member to an unnecessary shot "just to make sure" because we have kept no accurate record?

Get a record book and start now if you haven't before. To what drug did Susie react violently? When did the children last have their immunizations? What hereditary diseases are there in the family? Who has had x-rays and when? When were teeth last checked? What communicable diseases have the children had? When did they have them? You'll be glad to have your family's medical history handy if an emergency arises. It could save someone's life.

Family History

Several friends of mine have written extensive family histories to preserve for posterity. What an excellent way to keep memories, traditions, and family influences alive! Most of us regard such an undertaking beyond our capabilities, but we can still preserve family history through carefully kept photograph albums and baby books.

For years I kept family pictures in a cardboard box in the closet. We seldom looked at them because it was such an effort to wade through the disorder. Finally I decided to organize our pictures. I bought albums for each of our three boys and one for my husband and me. The unsightly box is gone, and our boys have their own family pictures.

Be sure to write under the pictures the name, date, and place. Your descendents will appreciate that. I have some pictures of people I presume are relatives but don't have the faintest idea where they belong on our family tree.

Keep up your baby books, too, otherwise you'll forget those important firsts and many of the cute things your children did. Children cherish their baby books, especially after they have grown up and have babies of their own.

Financial and Household

Keeping accurate financial records is essential, especially at income tax time. It's also handy to keep a record of various household details:

> date drapes were cleaned
> date carpet shampooed
> date oven cleaned
> date typewriter oiled and type of ribbon used
> seeds that produced the best carrots
> amount of sugar used when peaches canned

I also keep a record of letters I write, books I read, and guests I have entertained (for a pastor's family, the latter is tax deductible). The records will vary with each family, but all will appreciate the information at his fingertips when needed.

Spiritual Pilgrimage

I started keeping a diary when I was a little girl and faithfully recorded daily such interesting details as "got up, made bed, did dishes," and so on. My current diary isn't greatly improved, but I do enjoy looking back to compare the weather and family activities from year to year. At their best my diaries are of interest only to me.

A spiritual diary is much more important, however. Not only does it benefit me as I record the insights God gives me from His Word, but it is a legacy I can pass on to my children. We mimeographed my mother-in-law's "Grandmother's Thoughts" and gave them to her children and grandchildren shortly before she died. It was her last message to those she loved.

I too would like to leave a message for my children, grandchildren, and great-grandchildren. Therefore I keep a notebook for thoughts that come to me as I have my daily time with God. That way I don't lose the precious insights I glean from God's Word. I also record lessons I have learned and answers to prayer. They encourage me as I review them in times of discouragement or trial. I hope they will encourage and instruct my children and grandchildren after me.

Why not record your spiritual pilgrimage this year? It's an adventure all its own.

FAMILY DEVOTIONS

BIBLE STUDY: LOOK BACK, LOOK AHEAD

Talk about the blessings of the past year. Let each member recall times of God's protection, intervention, and provision in times of need. Discuss the difficult times of the preceding year and how God worked the difficulties together for good (Romans 8:28). You may even discuss failures and lessons that were learned through them. Stress God's forgiveness of our past failures and sins. If they have been confessed and forsaken, we can start the new year with a clean page.

Discuss answers to prayer during the past year.

Trace the ways God has led you during the past year as a family and as individuals. God tells us in Deuteronomy 8:2, "And you shall remember all the way which the Lord your God has led you." Joshua said, "Not one word of all the good words which the Lord your God spoke concerning you has failed" (Joshua 23:14).

Do you make New Year's resolutions? I prefer to set goals. There's something about a brand new year that inspires goal-making. What do you hope to accomplish in the coming year? What do you intend to learn?

Talk about goals with your family. Decide on family goals. They might include finishing the construction of the fence, planting, caring for and harvesting a garden, memorizing four psalms together, or sponsoring a refugee family. There are endless possibilities.

Talk about individual goals. Start by telling your children what yours are as parents.

Here are some possibilities:

    Dad: read the Bible through
        start and continue a weekly "family night"
        save two thousand dollars
        walk or jog regularly at least every other day
    Mom: lose ten pounds
        start a home Bible study
        read two inspirational books every month
        invite guests over for a meal or coffee at least twice a month
    Bobby: earn money for a new bike
        earn promotions in Boys' Brigade or Scouts
        read a few verses from the Bible every day
    Susie: keep room neat
        do Sunday school lesson regularly
        finish Piano Book II
        make a new friend

Look up and explain the following verses that will help in achieving goals: Matthew 17:20, 18:19-20; Luke 16:10, 18:27; John 15:7; Philippians 4:13.

Memory Verse: "Have I not commanded you? Be strong and courageous! Do not tremble or be dismayed, for the Lord your God is with you wherever you go" (Joshua 1:9).

Tiny Tot Verse: "The Lord your God is with you" (Joshua 1:9).

HYMN STORY: SONG FOR THE NEW YEAR

Fanny Crosby became blind at the age of six weeks. An ignorant doctor prescribed the wrong treatment for her inflamed eyes; her vision was destroyed. Instead of becoming bitter against that doctor, though, Fanny thought of him as an agent of God who equipped her for high and noble achievement. She was determined not to indulge in self-pity but be content with what she believed to be God's will for her. She even considered herself to be more fortunate than others, for the first thing she would see when her sight was restored in heaven would be her Savior's face.

Fanny Crosby wrote over eight thousand gospel songs. "All the Way My Savior Leads Me" is especially appropriate for the first month of the new year. Learn the song together. Borrow a hymnbook from your church if you do not know the tune.

All the Way My Savior Leads Me

All the way my Savior leads me;
  What have I to ask beside?
Can I doubt His tender mercy,
  Who through life has been my Guide?
Heavenly peace, divinest comfort,
  Here by faith in Him to dwell!
For I know what-e'er befall me,
  Jesus doeth all things well,
For I know what-e'er befall me,
  Jesus doeth all things well.

All the way my Savior leads me,
  Cheers each winding path I tread,
Gives me grace for every trial,
  Feeds me with the living bread.
Though my weary steps may falter,
  And my soul athirst may be,
Gushing from the Rock before me,
  Lo! a spring of joy I see,
Gushing from the Rock before me,
  Lo! a spring of joy I see!

All the way my Savior leads me;
  Oh, the fullness of His love!
Perfect rest to me is promised
  in my Father's house above.
When my spirit, clothed immortal,
  Wings its flight to realms of day,
This my song through endless ages:
  Jesus led me all the way;
This my song through endless ages;
  Jesus led me all the way.

Explain the meaning of the words to your children as you memorize it together. Jesus leads us in tender mercy; He does all things well; He is with us through our life-journey and will take us to heaven at last.

Memory Verse: "I will instruct you and teach you in the way which you should go. I will counsel you with My eye upon you" (Psalm 32:8).

Tiny Tot Verse: "He leads me" (Psalm 23:2).

A HERO TO FOLLOW: HE OPENED UP AFRICA

David Livingstone had to get up very early to go to work at the cotton mill in the town of Blantyre, Scotland, where he lived.* His job was to find and repair broken threads. David began doing that when he was only ten years old. After working fourteen hours every day, he attended night school.

When David was twenty-three years old he went to college in Glasgow where he prepared to become a missionary. He learned not only the Bible but medicine as well. At first he thought he would go to China, but since there was a war going on there he was sent to South Africa instead.

When David Livingstone reached Africa he began to do what most missionaries did in those days—preach the Gospel and treat the sick. But he saw "the smoke of a thousand villages to the north." He knew there were thousands of villages beyond the field he was working in. Who would tell all those people about Jesus?

David Livingstone decided that God wanted him to be an explorer-missionary. He would take a few natives with him into the interior and break a trail for others to follow. He would go first to the west, then to the east, and eventually to the north. He would open up the entire continent for the gospel as well as for commerce.

Livingstone was not a big man. He was only five feet, six inches tall and not very husky. But he was the kind of person who didn't let anything stop him from accomplishing his goals. He didn't give up.

It took many months for Livingstone to make those trips across the continent of Africa. As he traveled, he made maps and recorded important information about the country and its people. He discovered lakes, rivers, and mountains as he pressed on and on. He wrestled with hostile

* Adapted from *Junior Trails*, Gospel Publishing House. Used by permission.

tribes, malaria, hunger, wild animals, and wicked slave traders as he made his way through the dense jungles and grasslands.

After sixteen years in Africa he returned to England for a rest. He was surprised when everyone in his homeland treated him as a national hero. He was even asked to appear before the queen. He said to her, "Now I can tell my Africans I have seen my chief, and do you know what they will ask me? They will ask, 'How many cows has she?' " The queen laughed.

David Livingstone, though treated like a famous explorer, was a missionary at heart. The reason for his explorations was to prepare the way for missionaries to tell people about Jesus Christ.

Livingstone spent most of his life in Africa. He was getting old and was sick from the many hardships he had endured when a friend from America found him out in the jungle. Henry M. Stanley had been sent by the New York *Herald* to find Livingstone. Nobody had heard from him for three years, and he had heard from no one for five.

David Livingstone was very happy to see Mr. Stanley. His friend brought mail, news, and money for supplies. For four months he traveled with Livingstone, but he could not persuade him to return with him to civilization.

Stanley finally left him and returned home. Just a little over one year later, his native helpers found Livingstone dead on his knees beside his bed. His work for God and for Africa was done. Now it was time for a new generation to continue what he had started.

David Livingstone's favorite Bible verse was the promise of Christ in Matthew 28:20: "Lo, I am with you always, even to the end of the world." When native helpers betrayed him, when he met with fierce enemies, sickness, and fatigue, when his wife died, when he lay dying all alone of his last illness on the dark African trail, he claimed this glorious promise of Christ's presence: "It is the word of a gentleman of the most strict and sacred honor, so there's an end of it," he said.

There is also a task for you to accomplish, worlds to conquer, multitudes to tell of Christ. Christ's promise is also for you. He will be with you as He was with David Livingstone. Will you dare to go forward in His strength?

Questions for Thought:

1. At what age did David Livingstone began to work fourteen hours a day in the cotton mill in Scotland?

2. What was David Livingstone's dream after being in Africa for some time?
3. What hard things did he endure?
4. Why didn't David Livingstone give up?

Memory Verse: "Lo I am with you always, even to the end of the age" (Matthew 28:20).

Tiny Tot Verse: "I am with you always" (Matthew 28:20).

NATURE'S CORNER: HARDEST WORKERS OF THE INSECT WORLD

You may think you work hard, but have you ever watched a busy little ant?* There are any number of jobs to be done in the ant colony: building, gardening, shepherding, harvesting, cooking, and mothering.

Let's peek into an anthill and watch the ant baby-sitters. They take excellent care of their charges who are in various stages of development. When an anthill is uncovered, the nurses don't scurry away to protect themselves. No, they rush frantically to carry the eggs, babies, and white cocoons to safety in an underground room. The devoted baby-sitters give their charges baths with their tongues, feed them, and even take them out for walks on a fine day.

These scurrying creatures carrying grains of sand are the builders of the ant colony. They build their homes with many rooms, some of which are one thousand times as tall as themselves! They also construct roads, tunnels, and bridges that are amazingly strong in spite of the fact that the builders have no blueprints. (They don't even have brains!)

You may not recognize the ant gardeners. That piece of leaf they carry over their backs isn't an umbrella. Back in their earthen cave they chew the leaf, converting it into a green paste. Then they spread the substance on the walls and floor of their cave, and presto—they have a garden plot where they can grow mushrooms. The ants don't eat the mushrooms, but they love the tiny crystal grapes that form on them. The gardeners keep busy tending the mushrooms and picking the luscious grapes.

If you look closely you'll notice that some of the other ants scurrying into their hills are carrying something. They are the farmers busy with

---

* Adapted from *Treasure*, American Sunday School Union. Used by permission.

their harvest. One crew is on the top of grass stems gnawing off grass seeds, which fall to the ground. The ants on the ground gather them up and take them to their granaries. Because seeds sprout in a cool, dark place, the ants gnaw off the root-making part of the seed, called the radicle. The grass seeds make up an important part of the ants' diet and are sometimes called ant rice.

Ants in Texas, being a little more ingenious than those in other parts of our country, grind up the ant rice into ant flour. Their millers are soldier ants who grind-the seeds with their hard heads. The flour is taken to the ant kitchens where the cooks mix it with saliva and make it into little loaves of ant bread. The loaves are then carried out to bake on a stone in the hot Texas sun.

Speaking of Texas, did you know that there are also cowboy ants? The ants' cows are plant lice called aphids that give off a drop of sweet fluid when tapped on the back by an ant's feeler. The ants build special stables for their "cows" in underground tunnels, safe from thieves. During the winter they feed them plant roots. In the summer the ant cowboys take them out to pasture on the green leaves in someone's garden.

Ants are tidy and keep their colonies clean. Dead ants are immediately carried off to the cemetery. Garbage is disposed of quickly.

Nobody in the anthill complains about having to work too hard, not even the ant soldiers who protect the colony from enemies and occasionally make raids on other colonies to capture slaves.

Ants are the most industrious of all the insects. This is what the Bible says about ants. "Go to the ant, O sluggard, observe her ways and be wise, which, having no chief, officer or ruler, prepares her food in the summer, and gathers her provision in the harvest" (Proverbs 6:6-8).

Questions for Thought:

1. What are some of the jobs ants have?
2. How can ants do all those things?
3. What can you learn from ants?

Memory Verse: "Therefore be careful how you walk ... making the most of your time, because the days are evil" (Ephesians 5:15-16).

Tiny Tot Verse: "Making the most of your time" (Ephesians 5:16).

ACTIVITIES

Remember the old-time parlor games? Here are a few your children will enjoy playing with you. They're fun when you have company, too, especially other families with children.

Take a Picture
A and B know the secret, but nobody else does. A goes out of the room and B uses a spoon to "take a picture" of someone in the room. B then sits down in the same position as the person whose picture he has taken. (He will have to change that position if the person changes his position.) When A comes back into the room he looks in the spoon, but also looks at B to discover how he is sitting. Then he scans the other players. When he guesses correctly, everyone will be amazed.

Which Magazine?
Put nine magazines on the floor in rows of three. Send your partner (who knows the secret) out of the room. Ask one of the others to choose one magazine. Call your partner back in. Using a yardstick or other pointer, point to any magazine but the correct one and ask your partner, "Is it this one?" He will answer no and will know which one was picked. The secret is this: If, for example, the magazine in the lower left corner was chosen, put your pointer in the lower left corner of the first magazine you point to. Point to several other magazines before pointing to the right one.
Your partner will have no problem identifying it, but your guests will be mystified. If you keep playing, however, some of the rest will be sure to catch on. Then let them try.

Indoor Croquet
This could be a family project during an evening together, or it could occupy an afternoon when the weather is too bad to play outside. Making this miniature croquet set to be played on the dining room table will be as much fun as playing the actual game.

    Needed: 4 small spools
              2 tall thin spools
              9 pieces of wire
              4 long thin nails
             18 pieces of cork

4 marbles of different colors

Bend the wire into arches and put each end in a cork. Make mallets from the small spools and nails, painting each mallet to match a marble. The tall thin spools, painted with the colors, serve as posts. The marbles are used as balls. The rules are the same as for outdoor croquet.

If you wish to play on the floor you will need longer wires for the arches and small hammers wound with colored yarn for the mallets. Crayoned golf balls can be substituted for marbles. Fun for everyone!

Geography Guess

Two people must know the secret to this game. A goes out of the room. B asks the other players which geographical location (city, river, mountain, country) they would like to choose. Suppose they choose Cincinnati. He then calls A in and begins to question him. "Is it the Rocky Mountains? Is it San Francisco? Is it Japan? Is it Turkey? Is it Cincinnati?"

A will guess Cincinnati, much to everyone's amazement. The secret is to use a place with an animal in the name just before the correct answer. For example: Moosejaw, Deer Lodge, Catskill Mountains, Beaverlodge. You will think of more.

A continues to go out until one of the players thinks he has caught on and wants to try it.

A Nutty Game

Dad can ask the questions, and the other family members write the answers on slips of paper numbered from one to twelve, or they can call out the answers.

Which nut has in its name—
    The piece of a house? (walnut)
    Two boys' names? (filbert)
    A wooden box? (chestnut)
    The name of a country? (brazil)
    A vegetable? (peanut)
    A word for everything? (almond)
    A container? (pecan)
    A girl's name? (hazel nut)
    A kind of drink? (coconut)

A flower? (sunflower seed nut)
A good place to go on a hot day? (beechnut)
A spread for bread? (butternut)

My Grandmother Went to Paris

Mom can start this game. She says: "My grandmother went to Paris and with her she took a monkey" (or something else that starts with "M" for Mom). Dad continues: "My grandmother went to Paris and with her she took a monkey and a dragon" (or something that starts with "D"). Bobby says: "My grandmother went to Paris and took with her a monkey, a dragon, and a ball." By the time each family member has a second turn the list is getting long and hard to remember, but it's fun and a good memory exercise. See how long you can make the list.

Month Game

Players sit around the table. The leader points to one person, says the name of a month, and counts to ten. The one pointed at must give a fact about that month before the number ten is reached or he becomes "It." Facts for January can be: the first month, New Year's, coldest month, Susie's birthday, etc.

Family Projects

One family I know enjoys being together in the same room working individually on favorite projects. Dad makes a crackling fire in the fireplace; Mom turns on good classical or sacred music; each family member brings his own project, and they enjoy the fire and music together while working on their individual hobbies.

SOURCES

Ruth Bartlett, *Insect Engineers* (New York: William Morrow and Co., 1957).

George Douglas, *American Book of Days* (New York: H.W. Wilson Co., 1937).

Howard V. Harper, *Profiles of Protestant Saints* (New York: Fleet Press Corp., 1968).

Basil Miller, *Singing I Go* (Grand Rapids: Zondervan, 1950).

2

February

In the old Roman calendar, February was the last month of the year, a time for getting ready for the new year. A great deal of purification and cleansing took place. Could that be the forerunner of our modern spring cleaning?

An otherwise dreary month, February is brightened by the birthdays of two of our most admired presidents and by Valentine's Day with parties, heart-shaped cookies, and cherry desserts.

Valentine's Day is a combination of holy day and holiday. Valentine was a Christian in early Rome at a time when being a Christian was not only unpopular but also dangerous. As a doctor, he spent his time going about helping others, especially the despised Christians. For this "crime" he was imprisoned and later beheaded.

The Christians honored their beloved Valentine on the anniversary of his death which, curiously, coincided with the pagan festival of love and matchmaking, celebrated on February 14. Young girls drew names from a box to determine who their partner would be for the coming year. Gradually the two celebrations became one. Although Valentine's name graces the holiday, the man himself has been forgotten by most people. February 14 has become a day linked with romance and friendship, a time to send messages of love to sweethearts and friends.

In days past, girls hoped to find their mates on Valentine's Day. If a girl walked alone to a cemetery on Valentine's Day Eve, scattered a handful of hempseed, and sang a special song, she expected to find her true love following her home. Another method was to hardboil an egg, replace the yolk with salt, and eat it, shell included. If she could manage to do that and go to bed without speaking or drinking, the first man she saw in the morning would be her future mate.

Valentine cards gradually became popular in England, but sometimes they were used to express insults instead of love and friendship. Since the one receiving the mail paid the postage instead of the sender in early nineteenth-century England, a person who received an insulting valentine could demand his penny back from the postman.

Gifts became popular too: costly jewels, gloves, silk stockings, fancy garters. Sending a girl a pair of gloves was tantamount to a proposal of marriage, for the word *glove* contains the word *love*. If a girl wore the gloves to church, that meant she had accepted the proposal. Today most people settle for a valentine card, or sometimes a box of candy or flowers to express their love.

Valentine's Day is a good time to teach your children to give unselfishly as did Saint Valentine. It's a good day to spread love and cheer among the lonely and forgotten as well as to reassure family and friends of love and friendship. It is also an excellent time to teach your children about romance and marriage.

ESPECIALLY FOR PARENTS

Do you laugh a lot in your house?

The Bible tells us, "A merry heart doeth good like a medicine" (Proverbs 17:22). In his book entitled *Laughter and Health*, Dr. James J. Walsh recommends laughter to stimulate the organs of the body, improve circulation, and heighten resistance to disease. Laughter also stabilizes blood pressure, aids digestion, brings oxygen into the blood, and relaxes the body. Besides all those good things, it gives us a sense of well-being and improves our outlook on life. After you laugh, things don't seem as difficult as before.

Has your family had a good laugh lately?

A wife who was having marital problems said wistfully to me one day, "If only we could laugh together!"

Sometimes we are too uptight and tense to laugh—we explode instead, leaving ourselves and everyone else miserable. Relax and laugh a little. Your family will love it.

Children enjoy making grownups laugh. Don't groan at their jokes—

Why did the chicken cross the road? Oh no, not again—laugh at them! Tell a joke or two of your own. Jokes, even if corny, are far better than arguments.

Avoid jokes about God, heaven, hell, and Satan, or your children might think lightly of these realities. Avoid racist jokes, too—they do more harm than you think. Jokes about sex demean that God-given function making it seem coarse and sordid. Vulgar jokes should have no place in our homes. "Fools make a mock of sin" (Proverbs 14:9).

Laughing at people is a common pastime. How we must grieve God when we ridicule those He has created. Our children quickly catch on to laughing at others if they hear us do it.

Better to laugh at oneself. My oldest sister, Mabel, was an expert at that. When I was in the first grade I had to wear some old-fashioned, hand-me-down, hightop button shoes to school. They still had lots of wear in them, so my thrifty parents insisted I take my turn at wearing them.

I hated those shoes because my classmates laughed at them. A girl named Eloise was the worst offender. I came home in tears after she had teased me about my shoes.

"Don't cry," said Mabel, "just laugh with them. That's what I do when they tease me about my big lunch sacks. I just tell them I'm going to bring a gunny sack tomorrow."

I wished I could be like my big sister!

"When they tease you," she went on, "just laugh. Tell them you really love your shoes, that you put them in a special box every night. They'll soon stop teasing you."

I followed Mabel's advice, and it turned out exactly as she had said. Eloise stopped teasing me when I laughed with her. I found out that when you laugh at yourself others laugh with you not at you.

What about practical jokes? They can be fun for the family if not carried too far. Salt in the sugar bowl on April Fool's Day was a bit distressing, but we finally laughed with our Joe when we quit coughing. It wasn't as easy to be a good sport when my three small sons dangled a garter snake over my face one Sunday afternoon when I was taking a nap, but we laugh about it now.

It's fun to tell the children about amusing things they did when they were small, such as the time Tim comforted his newborn baby brother by letting him suck on his dirty big toe. And the time Joe promised to "pick a star" for his little friend on his first plane ride. Mark once asked after being brought inside to get cleaned up for church on a Sunday evening, "When we get to heaven we won't have to change clothes and go to church, will we?"

Maybe a collection of memories to laugh about would be more valuable to your family than a collection of salt and pepper shakers or Hummel figurines.

Go ahead, laugh a little.

FAMILY DEVOTIONS

BIBLE STUDY: MARRIAGE (2 CHRONICLES 18:1, 21-23)

It is never too early to start teaching your children the importance of marrying a Christian. This Bible story shows what happened when God's people disobeyed Him in this matter.

Jehoshaphat, king of Judah, was a good ruler. He not only followed God himself, but he taught his people to follow Him. God blessed Jehoshaphat, and he became strong and rich.

But Jehoshaphat made a big mistake. He arranged to have his son marry the daughter of wicked King Ahab and Queen Jezebel. Perhaps Jehoshaphat thought his son, Jehoram, would influence his new bride, Athaliah, to follow the Lord. Instead, the opposite happened. The daughter of Ahab influenced Jehoshaphat's son to forsake God and worship idols.

Not only did Jehoram forsake the Lord himself, but he also led his people away from God. He reigned only eight years, after which he died from a dreadful disease.

Athaliah's mischief did not end with her husband's death. She influenced her son, who became king in his father's place, to live wickedly. When he died, Athaliah decided that she wanted to become the ruler of the land. She destroyed all of her grandsons except one who escaped. Can you imagine your grandmother trying to kill you?

Wicked Queen Athaliah reigned over Judah for six years until the grandson who had escaped came out of hiding and took the throne. Athaliah was finally put to death but not before she had done a great deal of harm in Judah.

Questions for Thought:

1. How did it all start?
2. What does God say about this in 2 Corinthians 6:14?

3. What could happen in your family if you married an unbeliever?
4. Read 1 Kings 11:1-6 concerning Solomon's heathen wives turning him away from God.

Hold hands and pray together about the future mates of your children.

Memory Verse: "Do not be bound together with unbelievers; for what partnership have righteousness and lawlessness, or what fellowship has light with darkness?" (2 Corinthians 6:14).

Tiny Tot Verse: "Keep the commandments" (Matthew 19:17).

A HERO TO FOLLOW: A LOVE STORY

Hudson Taylor was a missionary to China over 100 years ago. He worked very hard to learn the Chinese language and to tell the Chinese people about Jesus Christ.

Sometimes Hudson Taylor felt lonely. He needed a wife to be his companion and helper.

In the city of Ning-po there lived a young English girl named Maria Dyer. She was lonely, too. Her parents had both died, and she and her sister had come to China with a lady missionary to help in a girls' school. Maria's sister had recently married, leaving Maria more lonely than ever.

Then she met Hudson Taylor, who sometimes came to her city on mission business. Every time she saw him she admired him more. Hudson felt the same about her. After one of their visits he wrote her a letter asking her to marry him.

Maria was overjoyed when she read the letter, but Miss Aldersey, the missionary she worked with, was not. How dare Hudson Taylor propose marriage to Maria! He wasn't good enough for her! Angrily, she ordered Maria to write the young missionary a letter of refusal, dictating what Maria was to write.

Maria felt she had to obey the woman, but she was heartbroken. She very much wanted to marry Hudson Taylor, but how would he ever find out how she felt?

Hudson was bewildered and hurt by the letter of refusal from the girl he loved, but he still did not give up. He prayed to God to yet give him Maria as his wife.

Maria prayed, too. If only they could meet privately so she could tell him of her love for him, but a private meeting was out of the question. In those days in China, young people of opposite sexes never met together unless chaperoned. To make it even more difficult, Miss Aldersey would make sure such a meeting never took place.

Hudson and Maria both asked God to take care of the difficulties. Strangely, it was a heavy rainstorm that finally brought them together. Hudson took refuge in a missionary's home to get out of the downpour. To his delight, the girl he loved had taken refuge in the same house. They had enough time together for Maria to assure Hudson that she did love him and wanted to marry him.

Overjoyed, Hudson wrote to Maria's guardian in England for permission. Mail was slow those days; it took months for the answer to come back, but when it came it was "Yes." In two months Hudson and Maria were happily married. They trusted God to work things out for them even when everything looked impossible. He didn't let them down.

He will work out His plan for you, too. Here are some good verses to find and read: Psalm 37:4-5, 7; Jeremiah 29:11; Romans 8:28.

Questions for Thought:

1. To what country did Hudson Taylor go as a missionary?
2. What prevented him from courting Maria?
3. What did he do about it?
4. How did God solve the problem for him?
5. What does this teach us?

Thank God together for His plan for each of His children and for His ability to work out that plan.

Memory Verse: "Trust in the Lord with all your heart, and do not lean on your own understanding. In all your ways acknowledge Him, and He will make your paths straight" (Proverbs 3:5-6).

Tiny Tot Verse: "Trust in the Lord" (Proverbs 3:5).

NATURE CORNER: THE PENGUIN FAMILY

Did you know that Emperor Penguins have no nests where they can raise their young? There is no material from which to build nests in the Antarctic ice cap where they live. Ice covers everything.

Mama Penguin lays her egg (only one a year) on the ice, which is not a very good place for eggs at all. It doesn't stay there long, however. Papa Penguin immediately rolls the egg into a fold of skin just above his webbed feet. The fat of his abdomen keeps the egg cosy warm.

After she has laid her egg, Mama Penguin leaves for the open sea. Papa Penguin, living on the food stored up in his body during the summer months, stays on the ice and "egg-sits." The temperature sometimes drops to seventy degrees below zero and frigid winds blow harshly. Papa Penguin has no shelter; however, as the weather becomes colder he seeks the company of other papa penguins. They huddle together much like a football team with their backs to the wind, gaining a little warmth from one another.

Meanwhile, Mama Penguin is having a feast of fish in the open sea. She eats and eats. Exactly two months after she has laid her egg on the ice she returns, just as the egg is about to hatch. Now it is her turn to baby-sit. She shelters the newly-hatched chick in the folds of her skin while Papa Penguin goes off to the sea for food.

Mama Penguin vomits up partially digested fish from her stomach for the baby bird. When Papa Penguin has eaten as much as possible, he returns and helps feed the baby in the same way. Papa and Mama Penguin will not have another meal for about a month, when the ice breaks up.

Isn't it wonderful that God has taught animals to adapt to their surroundings? He wants us to adapt to ours, too, even if sometimes they are unpleasant. Just as He supplies what the penguin family needs, so He also takes care of our needs.

Questions for Thought:

1. Where does Mama Penguin lay her egg?
2. What does Papa Penguin do with the egg?
3. Why does Mama Penguin go to the sea for two months?
4. What does Mama Penguin do to protect the newly-hatched penguin?
5. Who teaches the penguins how to adapt to their surroundings?
6. How does this make you feel about God?

Thank God together for His wisdom and His care.

Memory Verse: "Casting all your anxiety upon Him, because He cares for you" (1 Peter 5:7).

Tiny Tot Verse: "He cares for you" (1 Peter 5:7).

HYMN STORY: "JESUS LOVER OF MY SOUL"

Charles Wesley wrote many fine hymns that have survived for over 200 years and are still being sung today. One of his best loved hymns is "Jesus, Lover of my Soul." This beautiful song is credited with saving a soldier's life during the Civil War.

The event came to light one night when some tourists were sailing down the Potomac River. One of the group had a fine voice and was persuaded to sing for the others. The song he chose was "Jesus, Lover of my Soul."

After the song, a stranger came up to him and asked him if he had been in General Grant's forces during the Civil War eighteen years before. The singer affirmed that he had.

Had he fought in a certain battle?

Yes.

Had he sung "Jesus, Lover of my Soul" one night while on sentry duty?

Yes, the man remembered doing so. He had been feeling depressed when he went out for his guard duty. Lonely for home and friends, his thoughts turned to God and His care.

"I was a Confederate soldier," explained the stranger. "That night I had my gun aimed at you and was ready to shoot, but the words of your song stopped me. When you sang 'Cover my defenseless head with the shadow of Thy wing,' I didn't have the heart to shoot you. I lowered my gun and walked away. That song saved your life."

Jesus, Lover of My Soul

Jesus, Lover of my soul, Let me to Thy bosom fly,
While the nearer waters roll, While the tempest still is high.
Hide me, O my Savior, hide, Till the storm of life is past;
Safe into heaven guide, O receive my soul at last!

Other refuge have I none; Hangs my helpless soul on Thee;

Leave, ah, leave me not alone, Still support and comfort me.
All my trust on Thee is stayed. All my help from Thee I bring;
Cover my defenseless head with the shadow of Thy wing.

Plenteous grace with Thee is found, Grace to cover all my sin;
Let the healing streams abound; make and keep me pure within.
Thou of life the Fountain art, Freely let me take of Thee;
Spring Thou up within my heart, Rise to all eternity.

ACTIVITIES

Make Valentines

Making valentines is ever so much more fun than buying them! Provide your children with red construction paper, cardboard, lace, paper doilies, old greeting cards, scraps of cloth, rickrack, glitter, glue, scissors, and anything else you think will spark their creativity.

Make special snapshot valentines for family members or relatives. To do this cut a piece of cardboard to the desired size. Cover with a piece of red construction paper with a heart cut out of the middle. Insert and glue the snapshot under the heart-shaped opening. Glue rickrack around the edge.

For a very fancy snapshot valentine, make a cardboard frame edged with a lace ruffle. You will need to fasten the lace to the cardboard with straight pins and stiffen with a generous amount of white glue. Use waxed paper underneath for a minimum of mess. You can remove the pins after the lace sticks. When the frame is dry, glue your valentine to it.

An extra special valentine can be made out of an oatmeal box, using the cover and a cutdown portion of the box to make a trinket case. Glue cloth, preferably velvet, over the box and cover, leaving space for the cover to close. Glue on a favorite picture and trim edge with rickrack or lace.

Encourage your children to compose original verses to print on their homemade valentines.

Rhythm Band

Make your own instruments for a rhythm band. Make several instruments for variety.

Drum — Tape covers on oatmeal box or ice cream container.

Cover with contact paper or bright designs. Use fingers or dowels for sticks.

Tambourine — Lace tiny bells around a paper plate.

Trumpet — Hum through a paper towel roller.

Rattle — Fill baby food jars or covered soap dishes with dried beans and tape shut.

Blocks — Glue sandpaper on two small blocks of wood. Fit with handles.

Gong — Tie a string to a horseshoe and strike with a big nail.

Jingle Bells — Cover a piece of wood with cloth and sew on discarded bells.

Cymbals — Use two kettle lids.

Comb Instrument — Place a piece of paper over a comb and hum into it.

Xylophone — Fill six bottles with varying amounts of water and hit with a big nail. How about a solo?

Snare Drum — An old eggbeater whirring against a pan.

If a family member can play the piano, play a song your rhythm band can perform. If nobody plays, use a record or tape to carry the melody. Your toddler may opt to lead the band instead of playing an instrument.

Something to Grow

Cut off one end of a sweet potato and submerge the other end in water in a glass jar. Watch it grow.

Plant tomato seeds, petunia seeds, or others in boxes filled with dirt to transplant outdoors.

Balloon Fun

Blow up two balloons. Players sit across the room from each other and see how long they can keep the two balloons in the air. Players must stay seated on the floor as they hit the balloons with hands or feet. If both balloons hit the floor, the player nearest the last balloon to fall must share with the family something interesting that happened to him during the past few days or tell a joke. If the balloon drops near the same person several times, he may choose another person to share.

For small children, simply hit the balloons back and forth.

Simplified Scrabble

Put all the Scrabble squares on the table face down. Each player draws twelve squares, keeping them face down. At a signal each player turns over his squares and makes as many words as possible, crossword fashion. Letters must make words both vertically and horizontally. For example:

```
C A T
  O N L Y
  R
  L A N D
```

When a player uses all his letters, the other players must stop. The player with no letters left gets a zero score. All other players must add up the numbers on their unused letters. The player with the lowest score at the end of the game wins.

If your children are small, simplify it further by allowing them to make as many individual words as possible.

Valentine Cookies

Cut out and bake heart-shaped cookies together. Decorate with colored frosting. (*See* recipe in treat section.)

Tell children the story of Saint Valentine as they help roll out the cookies. Talk about sharing the cookies with a needy or lonely person (better double the recipe). Act out the story of Saint Valentine helping the Christians and ultimately being arrested and imprisoned. Parents, enter into the act, too. Your son or daughter would love to drag you off to prison.

SOURCES

Edna Barth, *Hearts, Cupids and Red Roses* (New York: Seabury Press, 1974).

Elizabeth Guilfoile, *Valentine's Day* (Champaign, Ill.: Garrard Publishing Co., 1965).

Lucy Kavaler, *Life Battles Cold* (New York: John Day Co., 1973).

Patricia Lauber, *Junior Science Book of Penguins* (New York: Scholastic Book Services).

Cecil Northcott, *Hymns We Love* (Philadelphia: Westminster Press, 1954).

Dr. and Mrs. Howard Taylor, *Hudson Taylor in Early Years* (London: China Inland Mission, 1911).

3

March

Moody March—a hint of spring in the air and some nice days, but also unpredictable stormy weather. Some of the worst weather in history—blizzards, floods, and earthquakes—has occurred in the month of March.

According to the old calendar, March was the first month of the year, but Julius Caesar changed it to the third. It was named after the god of war, Mars, whose symbol was the vulture. Mars was believed to be both vicious and cowardly, something like the changeable weather in the month named after him.

Only one holiday brightens this windy month (unless Easter falls in March): Saint Patrick's Day on March 17. Although this is a secular holiday in our country, it is a religious one in Ireland.

Did you know that Saint Patrick was not Irish? He was born in Scotland, the son of a Christian priest. One day when he was six years old, as the story goes, Patrick was playing by the seashore. Before he knew what was happening, a group of men appeared, seized him and forced him into a boat. His kidnappers were Irishmen who wanted Patrick as their slave.

Patrick spent the next years of his life in Ireland, working as a shepherd and waiting tables for his captors. During their wild pagan celebrations, he thought wistfully of his home and godly parents. If only he could return!

One night when Patrick was twelve years old, his wish came true.

During a feast when nobody was paying any attention to him, he quietly slipped away to the shore. Here the storytellers differ: some say he found a boat, others a hollowed out log at the water's edge. At any rate, with God's help, he made his escape safely across the water to his homeland and jubilant family.

Patrick often prayed for the Irish with whom he had lived for six years.

"I must go back to tell them about the true God," he said to his father.

Patrick's father sent him to school to train as a missionary. His education completed, Patrick returned to Ireland with a group of young men to teach his former captors of Christ. Many responded to his message and became Christians.

The grateful Irish elevated their missionary to sainthood and today celebrate his day with much fanfare.

When the Irish immigrated to the United States, they brought Saint Patrick's Day with them. In some places where the Irish are prominent there are parades and parties on Saint Patrick's Day. Most of us, however, honor the brave missionary simply by wearing something green.

Especially for Parents

Spring can be almost overwhelming. There are so many extra things that need to be done, not to mention the daily chores—spring cleaning, yard work, starting a garden, getting spring and summer clothes out for the children, plus numerous other tasks.

Life by the Inch

Do you feel swamped just thinking about it? Don't think about it as a huge mountain of work but as small jobs that can be done one at a time. Someone has said it this way: "Life by the yard is hard, but life by the inch is a cinch."

When we moved into a new house a few years ago, one of our big tasks was to put in a lawn. Before we could plant grass we had to clear the rocks away. There must have been a million of them! I felt totally overwhelmed with the greatness of that task until I decided to tackle it in small sections. I could clear one small section each day and finally it would all be finished. As I organized my huge task into small manageable parts, I was able to tackle the job with optimism.

"Life by the inch" works in bringing up our children, too. You wish you had more time to spend training and teaching them. So you don't have half an hour to give them a leisurely Bible lesson today, but you do have ten minutes to sit down with them and talk about the things that matter most. That's better than nothing.

Perhaps you can't teach them everything you would like to today, but you can teach them one thing. Maybe today you can teach them the importance of being kind to animals; tomorrow you can teach them something else. God taught His people: "precept upon precept; line upon line, here a little, and there a little" (Isaiah 28:10, KJV). That's how He teaches us, a little at a time, and we can do the same with our children.

Dad, you'd like to spend the evening at home with your family, but you must go to an important meeting. Perhaps you could find fifteen minutes before your meeting to roughhouse with your boys or read a story to your little girl.

Not everything—we live in a hectic, imperfect world—but something; maybe just an inch, but even an inch is progress.

Don't Be Listless

Don't approach your tasks in a listless manner. By that I mean, make lists. I write one list for tasks that must be done on a specific day such as vacuuming, baking a cake for the church supper, dusting, doing the laundry, picking up milk at the store, beginning my Sunday school lesson. Another list includes once-in-a-while jobs such as washing windows, cleaning closets, painting the bathroom. Then there are the list of "shoulds" such as: writing to a missionary friend, visiting a lonely relative, having a new neighbor over for coffee.

I make my lists according to priority. Some things obviously must be done, such as laundry and meal-making, while cleaning can wait if time runs out. Maybe a quick "pick-up" will do. Perhaps an oil change for the car is an absolute must while yardwork can wait until next week. Doing the necessary things first relieves us of pressure. We can work much more effectively when we are relaxed.

I derive much pleasure from crossing items off my list. It gives me a feeling of accomplishment and whets my appetite to do more.

Make lists as a family, and let family members choose which chores they will do. They'll enjoy crossing their job off the list when they have finished.

Use Scraps of Time

"A person's view of time is a way of discerning his personality," said a wise man. "Tell me what you think of time and I shall know what to think of you."

How often we lament our lack of time, not stopping to realize that God has given to each of us, rich and poor, young and old, well and sick alike, twenty-four hours every day, seven days every week, fifty-two weeks every year!

A wise person utilizes scraps of time. Put a long cord on your telephone so you can unload the dishwasher, set the table or peel potatoes for supper while talking on the phone. If I memorize Scripture or read while waiting for someone who is late I don't get nearly as upset at their tardiness.

Finish What You Start

The writer of Ecclesiastes said: "The end of a matter is better than its beginning" (Ecclesiastes 7:8). In other words, finish what you start.

ʼ Some people flit from one job to another, not finishing any of them. The result? Chaos. Better to complete a few jobs than start many and leave them unfinished. Finishing what we start before going on to something else eliminates confusion and frustration, two enemies of an organized household. It takes self-discipline, but the satisfaction of a job well done makes the effort worthwhile.

Teach your children this important principle. Encourage them not to quit in the middle of a project but to see it through to the end. The good habit of finishing what they start will help them succeed in life.

Secret

Do you know the secret of getting an unpleasant task done? This is really profound, so pay attention. Are you ready? Don't keep thinking about it and dreading it—*do it!*

FAMILY DEVOTIONS

BIBLE STUDY: JOSEPH (GENESIS 37-50)

The story of Joseph can be summarized in one evening's devotional time or told in detail in two or three evenings.

    I. Joseph as a Boy (Genesis 37:1-36)

    A. He is the favorite son

    B. He is hated by his brothers

    C. He is sold by his brothers

Discuss jealousy and sibling rivalry. Encourage honest sharing of feelings.

  II. Joseph as a Slave (Genesis 39:1-19)

    A. He is faithful

    B. He is promoted

    C. God is with him

    D. He refuses to sin

Discuss temptation. Encourage your children to be specific about temptations they face.

  III. Joseph as a Prisoner (Genesis 39:20—40:23)

    A. Does his best

    B. Given responsibility

    C. Interprets dreams

Discuss faithfulness: at home, at school, at work.

  IV. Joseph as Ruler of Egypt (Genesis 41:1—50:26)

    A. Interprets Pharaoh's dreams

    B. Saves Egypt and other nations from starvation

    C. Meets his brothers

    D. Forgives his brothers

    E. Welcomes his aged father

Discuss God's rewards for faithfulness. Discuss forgiveness. Discuss how God works all things together for good.

Questions for Thought:

1. Why were the brothers jealous of Joseph? (Genesis 37:3-11)
2. Who would you rather be, Joseph or his brothers, when Jacob saw the blood-stained coat? Why? (Genesis 37:31-36)
3. What was Joseph's secret of success when in Potiphar's house? (Genesis 39:2-3)

4. What did Joseph do when tempted to sin? (Genesis 39:12)
5. How do we know that Joseph didn't pout in prison? (Genesis 39:21-23)
6. Who gave Joseph the understanding of Pharaoh's dream? (Genesis 41:16)
7. What did Joseph say to his brothers when they found out who he was? (Genesis 45:4-13)
8. What did Joseph say to his brothers when they asked him to forgive them? (Genesis 50:19-21)
9. Read what Jesus says about forgiving others in Mark 6:14-15.
10. Can you think of someone you should forgive?

Have sentence prayers asking God's help to forgive a specific person and thanking God for His forgiveness.

Memory Verse: "And be kind to one another, tender-hearted, forgiving each other, just as God in Christ also has forgiven you" (Ephesians 4:32).

Tiny Tot Verse: "Be kind" (Ephesians 4:32).

A HEROINE TO FOLLOW: THE PRISONER'S FRIEND

Betsy's Quaker parents didn't know what to do with their daughter. In the late eighteenth century girls were expected to be quiet, demure, and well-behaved—especially Quaker girls. But Betsy was not like most Quaker girls. She was either laughing, whistling, singing, or dancing—always having fun. And how she loved bright colors, which was not pleasing to her Quaker elders who believed in dressing somberly.

The grownups who lived around Betsy believed she didn't have one serious thought in her head. How wrong they were! When Betsy was alone she thought of many serious things. For instance, she worried about dying. Every night she had the same dream: she was standing on a lonely shore hemmed in by the tide. The water rose higher and higher until it was about to drown her. Then she would awaken, only to have the same frightening dream the next night.

Betsy didn't have a very good opinion of herself. In her diary she calls herself "a bubble and a fool, all outside and no inside, a ship out at sea without a pilot."

All of that changed at a Quaker meeting one day. Betsy usually found the meetings unbearably dull. To amuse herself and her friends that day she wore purple shoes with red laces. But Betsy soon forgot about her outlandish shoes and even about her friends, as God spoke to her heart through the visiting Quaker preacher.

Betsy understood that even though she was like a bubble with no purpose in life, she did not need to stay that way. God loved foolish people, too. Jesus died for everyone, even her. Tears streamed down Betsy's face as she asked Jesus to forgive her sins and take over her life.

Betsy didn't have any more nightmares about drowning after that. She realized she no longer needed to fear death. She now belonged to God. He had saved her not only from her sin and its punishment but also from an empty life.

Later Betsy, whose real name was Elizabeth, married Joseph Fry. She became the mother of eleven children. Besides caring for her family, Elizabeth began a very special work that resulted in her becoming quite famous. She went to the prisons to read and explain the Bible to the prisoners.

In those days prisons in England were little more than dungeons. The prisoners, some yet unconvicted, were treated like wild beasts. Elizabeth Fry read to them of Jesus and His love. How happy the prisoners were to hear this message of hope. Many condemned people found forgiveness and new life in Jesus through Elizabeth's visits.

Elizabeth prayed with prisoners on their way to the gallows, comforted the sick, brought hope to the mentally ill, encouraged the despairing. She also went to the courts to plead for improvement in the prisons. Thanks to her efforts, the conditions in prisons in England, as well as other countries of the world, became better.

Elizabeth Fry's favorite Bible story was the one about Jesus loving and forgiving the woman who was such a great sinner. Jesus had also forgiven Elizabeth, so she wanted to spend her life sharing with others that Jesus came to save sinners, and He would save even the worst who came to Him.

Questions for Thought:

1. What dream did Betsy have as a girl?
2. What was she afraid of?
3. What good news helped her overcome this fear?
4. How did she share this good news with others?
5. Who can you share this good news with?

Have prayer to be used of God to help others.

Memory Verse: "Come to me, all who are weary and heavy-laden, and I will give you rest" (Matthew 11:28).

Tiny Tot Verse: "Come to me" (Matthew 11:28).

NATURE CORNER: SAMMY SNAIL

Sammy Snail does not need parents to care for him when he hatches from his shell.* The small pink creature with a thin, paper-like shell knows exactly what to do. As soon as he is hatched he begins to eat. The first item on his menu is the eggshell from which he has hatched. After he finishes that he begins to eat the tender leaves around him.

He knows that enemies are lurking about to finish him off, so he hides during the daytime. At night he moves about, eats, and grows.

Sammy cannot move quickly. You couldn't either if you had only one foot and were carrying your house on your back. Sammy does something remarkable when he walks—he lays down a carpet to slide over. It's a thin carpet of mucus which flows from his body. This carpet makes it easy for him to slide along. It also makes it possible for him to stick to surfaces, even when they go straight up, straight down, or when he is upside down.

Sammy Snail starts building his house right after he is born. His building material is simply a pasty fluid that flows from his body and forms a hard shell around him. As he grows he adds new spirals to his house, so he never has to look for a bigger one. He is never without shelter either, for he carries his house right along with him wherever he goes. He sticks his head and foot-belly out of his front door in order to look for food and to move about. If his eyes, mounted on two long tentacles on his head, see danger coming he retreats quickly into his house. Sometimes he feels or smells danger with a shorter pair of tentacles, but his shell is always handy for a hasty retreat.

Some snails have a horny door on the bottom of their foot which closes when they go inside. Sammy is the kind of snail that makes his doors as he needs them by blowing a mucous bubble in the opening of

* "Sammy Snail" was printed in *Discovery*, Light and Life Press, Winona Lake, Ind. in 1975 and is used by permission.

his shell, which flattens and hardens into a covering after he is safely inside.

If Sammy's house gets broken from a fall, he begins to repair it immediately. He has the materials for repair in his own body—the same supplies he used to build his shell in the beginning. The mending takes about two or three weeks, but Sammy never has been famous for speed.

He is small, but he is strong. He can pull an object 200 times his own weight. That would be like your walking down the street carrying a grand piano on your shoulders.

Sammy's mouth is small (you can't see it without a magnifying glass), but it contains over 25,000 teeth! The snail needs his tiny teeth to shred food. Sometimes he even eats limestone rocks. The limestone turns into calcium in his body. Sammy uses this calcium to add to his shell housing as well as to replace worn out teeth. No trips to the dentist for Sammy!

When cold weather comes, Sammy goes into his shell, makes a door to shut him in, and curls up and goes to sleep for the entire winter. He does the same thing in very dry weather. He can live for months without eating or drinking.

Many snails are captured by enemies. Wading birds, frogs, turtles, mice, snakes, and muskrats are always on the lookout for a juicy snail. The snail's greatest enemy, however, is man. Men gather snails for food. The people of France are the champion snail eaters, but many Americans relish snails also.

So far Sammy has escaped his enemies. He hides in the moist leaf mold of the earth and among the roots of grass. If he continues to escape from his enemies he will probably live about five years.

How does Sammy know what food to eat, how to build his house complete with that fancy door? How does he know how to repair his house, how to escape the heat and cold by hibernating in his shell? How does he know that he must quickly withdraw into his house and shut the door when he sights an enemy?

Scientists tell us that Sammy knows all that by instinct. But who gave him that wonderful instinct? The creator of the universe, of course. God, who made you, also made this remarkable little creature and many others that are equally amazing. What a wonderful, wise God He is.

Questions to Think About:

1. Why does Sammy move slowly?
2. What kind of a house does he live in?
3. Why doesn't he have to go to the dentist?
4. What does he do in cold weather?
5. Who made Sammy Snail so wise?

Lead your children in prayers of praise to God for His wonderful works.

Memory Verse: "Oh, the depth of the riches both of the wisdom and knowledge of God! How unsearchable are His judgments and unfathomable His ways!" (Romans 11:33).

Tiny Tot Verse: "He has made everything" (Ecclesiastes 3:11).

HYMN STORY: "IT IS WELL WITH MY SOUL"

About 100 years ago a family named Spafford lost their possessions in the great Chicago fire. In spite of this tragedy, they decided to go on the long-awaited vacation to Europe they had planned.

Mr. Spafford saw his wife and four children off on a luxury liner, intending to join them later. On the way to Europe, a British iron sailing vessel rammed the luxury liner. The ship went down. Among the 226 passengers that drowned were the four Spafford children.

As soon as possible, Mrs. Spafford cabled a message to her husband: "Saved—alone."

Mr. Spafford, heartbroken when he thought of his children, took the next ship to go to his grieving wife. As the ship he sailed on neared the place where his children had gone down, questions and doubts filled his mind. Why had this tragedy happened to his family?

For a time he struggled with these questions, but finally was able to turn them over to God. He remembered that God is love and that He is all-wise. Someday Mr. Spafford would understand why God took his children. Now he would simply trust God's love and wisdom.

Trusting brought peace to the sorrowing father. In his cabin he took paper and pen and wrote the words to the hymn, "It Is Well with My Soul." It tells us that we too can have peace, no matter what happens, if we trust in God.

It Is Well with My Soul

When peace, like a river, attendeth my way,
 When sorrows like sea billows roll;
Whatever my lot, Thou hast taught me to say,
 It is well, it is well with my soul.

Chorus:
It is well ... with my soul ...
It is well, it is well with my soul.

My sin—oh the bliss of this glorious thought—
 My sin—not in part, but the whole,
Is nailed to the cross and I bear it no more,
 Praise the Lord, praise the Lord, O my soul!

And, Lord, haste the day when the faith shall be sight,
 The clouds be rolled back as a scroll,
The trump shall resound and the Lord shall descend,
 Even so, it is well with my soul.

Memory Verse: "Peace I leave with you; My peace I give to you; not as the world gives, do I give to you. Let not your heart be troubled, nor let it be fearful" (John 14:27).

Tiny Tot Verse: "Let not your heart be troubled" (John 14:27).

ACTIVITIES

Family Drama
Children play-act from the time they are small, pretending to be parents, firemen, what have you. Encourage them to dramatize stories they know as well as make up skits of their own to entertain the family. Divide into two groups: each group performs a skit for the other. (Two in one group is enough; a child may play several parts.)

To aid in family dramas, fill a box with old clothes, discarded hats, purses, and shoes. Children love to dress up, and the costumes will enhance your family dramas.

This month, act out the story of Joseph that you have been studying. This will impress the story indelibly upon your children, as well as teach them to express themselves.

Homemade Games

Save items you usually throw away to make homemade games.

Toss. Cut an oatmeal box into round strips to use as rings. Turn a kitchen chair upside down and toss the rings at the legs. Keep score. Dad and Mom should stand farther away from the chair if they are competing with little ones.

Home Basketball. Roll up a pair of socks, and use them for a ball. Take turns throwing the ball into a clean wastepaper basket. Or fasten a bottomless milk carton to the wall and play basketball. (Our boys kept one of these taped to the wall in their bedroom and spent hours throwing their sock ball into it.)

Ring on a Rope. Put a ring on a heavy string or light rope. Sit in a circle with one family member "it." Pass the ring from one person to the other as secretly as possible. The person who is "it" stands in the center and tries to find the ring. When he does, the person who has it must become "it."

Button Magic. Take a large button (at least one inch in diameter) and put a sturdy thread through first one hole, then the other. Tie to secure. Holding an end of the string in each hand, throw button forward several times to wind string, then pull apart. The string becomes elastic. Continue to pull and release.

Clay Play. Here is the recipe for homemade clay:

1 c. flour
1 c. salt
1 T. powdered alum (available at drugstore)
1 c. water (increase or decrease to desired consistency)

Form clay into objects to paint and keep or give as gifts. The clay will harden by itself. To reuse, make into balls, wrap in a damp cloth, and store in an airtight container.

Small children will enjoy making worms, cookies, and fruit. Older children will be able to make bowls, vases, and animals. The possibilities are endless.

Outdoor Fun

Children will be eager to get outside during this month if the weather permits. If possible, plan early suppers so you will have enough light to play outdoors with your children before coming in for family devotions and refreshments. How about flying kites?

Jumping Contest. Put two sticks on the ground and see if your children can jump over them both. Start with the sticks close together, then move them farther apart to make the distance greater. See how far they can jump. When they're tired of that, see how high they can jump. Parents can hold a heavy string or light rope close to the ground, then raise it a little higher each time until the children can no longer clear the string.

SOURCES

F. W. Boreham, *A Temple of Topaz* (Philadelphia: Judson Press, 1928) pp. 213-222

George William Douglas, *American Book of Days* (New York: The H.W. Wilson Co., 1937) p. 141

Ernest K. Emurian, *Hymn Stories for Programs* (Grand Rapids, Mich.: Baker Book House, 1963) pp. 37, 38.

Lila Hess, *A Snail's Pace* (New York: Charles Scriber's Sons,1974) pp. 5-21

Oscar Shisgall, *That Remarkable Creature, the Snail* (New York: Julian Messner, 1970) p. 20

4

April

Some people think the name for our fourth month came from the Latin word *aperire*, meaning "to open." Leaves and buds begin to open in earnest during the month of April.

The first holiday of this month is April Fool's Day. It is believed that his holiday originated in France. Even though Julius Caesar had changed New Year's from spring to January 1, not everyone was willing to accept this change. The diehards continued to celebrate April 1 as their New Year's Day and because of this were teased by their friends and called "April fools." Gradually the first day of April became a day to trick people and have fun.

Don't be too serious to have fun with your children on this day if the joke is on you (for instance, sugar in the salt shaker).

The other holiday that usually falls in April is Easter, the resurrection day of our Lord. At first Christians celebrated Easter on various days, but always around the time of the vernal equinox. Since Constantine's time (fourth century A.D.) the date has been determined by an astronomical formula. This was decided upon by the Council of Nicaea.

It is believed that the word *Easter* came from "Eostre," the name of the ancient goddess of spring. Her symbols, dating from pre-Christian times, are the egg and the rabbit, which have somehow become a part of our Christian Easter celebrations.

Don't let the Easter bunny and the bright-colored eggs distract your children from the true meaning of resurrection day which is the corner-stone of our Christian faith and the greatest holiday of all!

ESPECIALLY FOR PARENTS

"Mom, company's coming!" I remember the thrill I felt when I saw a car coming up our long driveway on a Sunday afternoon. Company spelled excitement: something special to eat, interesting conversation, a glimpse into someone else's life, maybe even children my own age to play with.

Sometimes whole families would appear and stay for supper. My hospitable mother never seemed flustered. She always had homemade bread or rolls on hand, canned fruit in the cellar, some canned meat or fishballs, and the chocolate cake with white icing she made almost every Saturday.

Looking back, I feel that my parents' hospitality was one of their greatest gifts to me. I learned so much from the people that came into our home. Who can measure the influence of the godly pastors and missionaries who sat down at our table? No wonder three members of my family became missionaries.

We learned other things, too: to tolerate other viewpoints; to over-come shyness; to share what we had with others; to care for people outside of our family circle.

When my husband and I married, we endeavored to carry on the tradition of hospitality we had learned from our parents. Our three boys listened spellbound when a missionary told of his adventures in Africa. They were awed when a prisoner-turned-preacher related his experiences and how Christ had changed him. They understood a little of what it's like to be handicapped when we had a young blind friend over for dinner on Sundays. We dished up his food as if his plate were a clock: potatoes at three o'clock, meat at six, and vegetables at nine. They learned compassion when we invited a lonely, elderly relative to spend holidays with us. They had a great time when our guests were families with children. Their lives were enriched by the "company" we had in our home.

Hospitality Versus Entertainment

A cake mania spread across the United States during the years after the Civil War. A hostess might bake as many as twenty cakes for a party. Each guest was expected to sample them all! Lavish entertainment was the order of the day—whole animals were roasted out-of-doors and served with a variety of side dishes.

A Mrs. Bringhurst, a woman with a small appetite, rebelled at this overeating. She dared to break with convention and serve only coffee, cake, and ices at her parties. Gradually this simple way of entertaining became accepted. "Lap feasts" or buffet suppers were also initiated.

Today ten-course dinners and twenty-cake parties are unheard of except perhaps for the very rich or for very special occasions. Simplicity puts entertaining within everyone's reach. Invite your friends for meatballs or a casserole if you can't afford steak. If even that strains your budget, invite them for a potluck supper. Nobody minds bringing a salad or a dessert. Contributing something to the meal may even make them feel more at ease.

Entertainment can be a purely selfish venture—repaying someone who has entertained you or who you hope will have you back. Hospitality is much more: it is opening your heart as well as your home to people.

Our home is our refuge, part of ourselves. When we open it to others, we are giving them part of ourselves. I feel honored to be invited into someone's home, even if only for a cup of tea. I feel accepted.

Hospitality is opening our home to not only our special friends but also to strangers, non-Christian neighbors, foreigners in our country, the lonely and handicapped.

I was surprised when I first met Teresa, a young Korean woman, to learn that during three years in the United States she had never been invited into an American home until we invited her into ours. Teresa responded to our friendliness with warmth and listened to our witness of Christ. Although she moved away before becoming a Christian, several years later she wrote that she had finally yielded to Christ. She attributed her conversion to our hospitality, because, she insisted, that's where it all began.

When we moved into a new neighborhood I (rather fearfully, because I'm shy) knocked on my neighbors' doors and invited them for coffee. Most of them came quite gladly. That first get-together was a bit strained because I was a stranger to all of them, but it was the beginning of friendships and blossomed into a neighborhood Bible study. We have a wonderful time together now.

I get a special blessing from having our friend Walt over. He's a bachelor who seldom gets a home-cooked meal. He appreciates my cooking even when it's a flop. I never have to worry about leftovers when Walt comes for dinner.

Jesus instructs us not to prepare feasts for our friends who will return the favor, but for those who are not in a position to invite us back. He promises a special blessing for that kind of hospitality.

Children thrive in a home that is warm with hospitality. Don't wait until you have more skill, more money, or until you get the living room painted. Have somebody over now.

"Mom, company's coming!" Do the words send a chill up your spine? Relax. Be glad you can share the home God has given you. Swoop those newspapers off the floor and plug in the coffee pot.

FAMILY DEVOTIONS

BIBLE STUDY: ABOUT DEATH AND RESURRECTION

Children probably first encounter death when a favorite pet dies. They tearfully ask if their dog will go to heaven. Later they may experience the death of a loved one or friend. Some parents assure their children that their pet did indeed go to heaven. Some shield their children from the truth of death by not allowing them to attend the funeral of a relative or friend.

It is important to tell our children the truth about death; otherwise they may spend all their lives in the terrible bondage of fear. We fear the unknown, but because Jesus conquered death, His followers can look upon it as a defeated foe. Paul actually called death "far better" than earthly life and "gain" because it introduced him to the next life, which is so far above man's existence here that human expression cannot describe it.

Read the story of the crucifixion and resurrection of Jesus from the Bible to your children (Matthew 27 and 28), preferably in a modern version.

Questions for Thought

1. Do animals go to heaven? No, but you can describe God's beautiful plan for His creation to your children. This is a good time to explain that the difference between animals and people is that people are created in the image of God and have an eternal soul.
2. What happens to people who die? Use the illustration of an egg.

Crack open an egg. Explain that people are made up of body, soul, and spirit, just as an egg is made up of the shell, the white, and the yolk. Let the shell represent the body. Explain that at death the soul and spirit go to God if the person is a Christian. The body is put in the ground until the resurrection day when it will join the soul and spirit with Jesus. At that time it will be a new body that will never get sick or die. If you like, you can put the eggshell in a little box and bury it in the ground to illustrate how a person's body is buried.

When Jesus returns for His own, the Christian dead will arise with immortal bodies. Those bodies will be joined to the soul and spirit that are already with Jesus.

Read 1 Corinthians 15:51-57. Explain that you can't put the egg back together again, but God can put us back together again, giving us eternal, incorruptible bodies like the body Jesus had when He arose from the dead. Look at the following verses to see what His glorified body was like:

John 20:19—He could appear and vanish
Luke 24:40-42—He could eat
Acts 1:9—He ascended, defying gravity
1 John 3:2—We will be like Him

Another way to illustrate the resurrection is by planting a seed and watching it grow into a lovely plant with blossoms. Or put a caterpillar in a jar and watch it form its cocoon and finally emerge into a beautiful butterfly.

This may be a good time to explain to your children that they must have a personal faith in Jesus. *They* must decide whether or not they want to follow Him—their parents cannot decide for them. Lead them in a simple prayer of acceptance if they express a desire: "Jesus, forgive my sins. Thank You for dying on the cross for me. Come into my life. I want to someday go to live with You forever."

Memory Verse: "Because I [Jesus] live, you shall live also" (John 14:19).

Tiny Tot Verse: "He has risen" (Luke 24:6).

A HERO TO FOLLOW: WHAT HAPPENED TO ADONIRAM?

I suppose people thought Adoniram was a Christian because he was a PK (Preacher's Kid).* Everyone just naturally expects PKs to follow in their parents' footsteps. But you know as well as I do that having Christian parents, even those involved in full-time service, doesn't make you a Christian.

Adoniram was a brainy kid. You might even call him brilliant. He learned to read when he was three and stayed at the head of his class all through school.

In 1803, when Adoniram started attending Providence College, it was "in" to be a skeptic and pooh-pooh Christianity. Since Adoniram was a Christian in name only and not in heart, it was easy for him to go along with this popular idea. A brilliant skeptic one year older than Adoniram became his best friend and strengthened him in his unbelief.

By the time Adoniram had finished college he had no interest in the faith of his parents. You can imagine the ruckus that occurred when he went home with that announcement. His father had hoped young Adoniram would become a preacher. Instead, his son declared himself to be an atheist.

Adoniram left his heartbroken parents to begin a tour of the northern states on horseback. One night when he reined his horse at an inn the landlord explained that he had only one room available, and it was next to that of a dying man.

Adoniram cheerfully agreed to take the room. Death didn't bother him, he said. When he reached the room he found out he was mistaken. The dying man's groans kept him awake and disturbed him all night. The man seemed to be in agony. Adoniram began to think of what he had been taught as a child. Was it true after all that there was a God and there was life after death? Was there an eternity as the Bible taught?

In the morning as he prepared to leave the inn, Adoniram asked the landlord how the sick man was.

"Oh, he died," explained the man. "Too bad. He was a fine chap, a graduate of Providence College."

"Providence College!" gasped Adoniram. "What was his name?"

Upon hearing the dead man's name, he became pale. It was his skeptic friend! Adoniram suddenly realized he wasn't an unbeliever

---

* Adapted from *Encounter,* a Wesleyan Methodist publication. Used by permission.

after all. God was real, and eternity was real. His friend had gone into eternity unprepared—it was too late for him. Was it too late for Adoniram?

The young man mounted his horse and started for home. Something happened to him on that trip—the God of his parents became his God. Putting his faith in the atonement of Jesus Christ, he became an ardent believer.

Adoniram never did anything halfway. When he became a Christian he gave himself 100 percent to the Lord. He began to study for the ministry. The more he studied the more concerned he became for people in other lands who had no opportunity to hear of Christ. One day as he was walking in the field by himself, God seemed to speak directly to him with these words: "Go ye into all the world and preach the gospel to every creature" (Matthew 16:15).

At that time there were no foreign mission organizations in America. Adoniram banded together with a group of other young men who felt called to foreign missionary service to have a prayer meeting in the rain under a haystack.

That prayer meeting resulted in the formation of the American Board of Foreign Missions. This board agreed to send Adoniram to India.

Adoniram quickly married his young sweetheart, and together they sailed for India. The East India Company, which was in control of India at that time, did not want missionaries working in India, so they had to leave. Instead of returning to America, however, they took a ship to Rangoon, Burma. In that idolatrous country where foreigners were suspect and living conditions often unbearable, Adoniram and his young wife began their missionary work.

Adoniram built a small chapel by the roadside and preached to people as they traveled back and forth. It took seven years to win his first convert. Slowly, a few others came to Christ. Meanwhile he was translating the Bible into the Burmese language.

When war broke out between Burma and England, Adoniram was arrested as a spy and thrown into a horrible prison. For seventeen months he suffered there and almost died. His wife, Ann, slipped food to him whenever she could. When Adoniram was finally allowed to return to his home he found that his wife had taken ill and died. His child died soon after.

Adoniram did not give up, even in the face of these tragedies. After a thirty-three-year absence from the United States, he finally returned to tell his family and friends about what God was doing in Burma. While there the Lord gave him a second wife to return with him.

Adoniram Judson lived to see the Bible and other books translated into and published in Burmese. Schools were established to teach people to read. He left sixty-three churches, 7000 converts, and many fellow-workers.

What happened to Adoniram? He found that, in spite of what the skeptics said, God is real and eternity is real. Thousands of Burmese people will spend eternity with the Lord because Adoniram spent his life sharing this message with them.

Questions for Thought:

1. Why did people think Adoniram was a Christian?
2. What happened to him when he went to college?
3. Who arranged for him to have a room next to a dying man?
4. Who was the man and how did his death affect Adoniram?
5. Where did Adoniram Judson serve as a missionary?
6. Tell about some of the things he accomplished.
7. What did you learn from this true story?

Memory Verse: "Jesus said to him, 'I am the way, and the truth, and the life; no one comes to the Father, but through Me'" (John 14:6).

Tiny Tot Verse: "Jesus said . . . I am the way" (John 14:6).

NATURE CORNER: PRINCES AND KINGS

A baby peacock, or peabiddy, isn't much to look at.* Writer Flannery O'Conner said, "For the first two years of his life he might have been put together out of a rag bag by an unimaginative hand." He is a dull grey color at first, has long, awkward legs, and just a smidgeon of a tail. Gradually he begins to grow a brown crest, and green flecks appear on his neck. Little by little his tail grows, and the beautiful colors and markings appear. By the time he is three years old he looks like what he was born to be, the king of birds.

Words fail when a person beholds the peacock raising his gorgeous tail as a multi-colored arch about him. He seems to realize he is putting

* Adapted from *Reachout*, Light and Life Press. Used by permission.

on a show as he turns, struts, and bows. In the spring and summer when his tail is full and splendid, he struts for several hours in the morning, takes a rest during the midday heat, and struts again in the afternoon. By his strutting, dancing, and display of his feather fan, he hopes to attract a peahen.

Peacocks start acting like royalty soon after they are born. Though the small peabiddy is not beautiful and has no gorgeous tail to display, he raises his tiny, nondescript tail, and struts, turns, and bows like an adult peacock. Does he know that someday he too will have an indescribably beautiful feather fan and evoke the admiration of all who see him? Does he know he is a prince and will someday be the king of birds?

Peacocks have extremely aristocratic habits, such as eating flowers, preferably roses and chrysanthemums. If they aren't hungry, they merely pick them and let them drop. They often choose to make the flower bed into a dust bowl for taking their dirt baths. They hold court on fences and gates with no thought that their combined weight is making them sag and break down.

People in ancient times thought the peacock was divine, but not only because of his beautiful fan spread. The eye-like markings on his plumage, they believed, held magical powers for protection.

To early Christians, however, the peacock symbolized immortality. They adorned their churches with peacock feathers. The peacock was a symbol of the resurrection of the believer. The shedding of the peacock's feathers in late summer symbolized the death of the earthly body. Shortly after Christmas the peacock has regained his gorgeous plumage and feather fan. That symbolized the glorified body that the Christian receives at the resurrection. We can apply this analogy even today.

We may be very ordinary in our own estimation and in the estimation of others, just as ordinary as the unattractive peabiddy. But if we have received Jesus Christ, we are children of the King of Kings and Lord of Lords. If we are faithful Christians we too will someday be kings and reign with Him.

The peacock's gorgeous plumage won't compare to the glory that shall be ours when we receive our resurrected, immortal bodies.

I don't recommend strutting (that's for the birds!), but hold your head up high. Be happy. Be brave. You're a child of the King. You're a potential king. Unimaginable glory is waiting for you!

Questions for Thought:

1. What does a baby peacock look like?
2. Why do peacocks strut?
3. What did the peacock symbolize to the early Christians?
4. What does the peacock's gorgeous plumage remind us of?
5. To what do Christians look forward?

Memory Verse: "Beloved, now we are children of God, and it has not appeared as yet what we shall be. We know that, when He appears, we shall be like Him, because we shall see Him just as He is" (1 John 3:2).

Tiny Tot Verse: "We are children of God" (1 John 3:2).

HYMN STORY: "AMAZING GRACE"

John Newton's mother died when he was seven. He spent the next four years in a strict boarding school where he was most unhappy. When he was eleven years of age his father, a sailor, permitted him to go to sea.

John soon forgot the things his loving mother had taught him about God and right living. He refused to obey those over him, so he got into one scrape after another. He began to even make fun of God and influence others to do so. Going deeper and deeper into sin, he ended up as a slavetrader.

But God loved John and kept after him. In the same way that He sent a storm to speak to disobedient Jonah, so He sent a storm to speak to John. John worked hard at the pumps to save the ship, but he was sure the vessel would go down and that he would drown.

Then John Newton began to pray to the God he had ridiculed. God heard him and mercifully saved the ship from going down, while also saving John from his sins. John Newton became a new man as he believed in and followed Jesus. The twenty-three-year-old later became a preacher and a hymnwriter. He was so grateful for what God had done he wrote a song about it called "Amazing Grace." Grace simply means that we are given God's love and forgiveness even though we don't deserve it.

Amazing Grace

Amazing grace! how sweet the sound,
    that saved a wretch like me!
I once was lost, but now am found,
    was blind, but now I see.

'Twas grace that taught my heart to fear,
    and grace my fears relieved;
How precious did that grace appear
    the hour I first believed!

Through many dangers, toils and snares,
    I have already come;
'Tis grace hath brought me safe thus far,
    and grace will lead me home.

When we've been there ten thousand years,
    bright shining as the sun,
We've no less days to sing God's praise
    than when we first begun.

Question for Thought:
When we believe in Jesus, what does God give us that we don't deserve?

Memory Verse: "For by grace you have been saved through faith; and that not of yourselves, it is the gift of God" (Ephesians 2:8).

Tiny Tot Verse: "Saved through faith" (Ephesians 2:8).

ACTIVITIES

Let's Have Company! Your children will enjoy planning an evening with friends (preferably another family or two with children). They will learn the art of hospitality as you plan for the food and games together.

A potluck supper is easy because the guests contribute food. Or why not simply invite your friends over for dessert? Sundaes are popular, especially if there are a number of toppings to choose from and chopped nuts to sprinkle on top. Maybe a popcorn party would be fun.

Before eating, lead in a prayer of thanksgiving, not only for the food but for family, friends, and fun. You may even want to share one of the devotionals or sing a song together.

Games

Rhythm. This game can be enjoyed by young and old alike. Sit in a circle on chairs. Number the players. The object of the game is to get to the head of the circle.

Number One should be adept at the game and able to establish a four-beat rhythm. He slaps his knees with both hands, then claps his hands, snaps his fingers, claps his hands again and starts all over by slapping his knees once more. As he snaps his fingers he says a number. The person with that number must then call out a number himself when the next snapping of the fingers occurs, all the while keeping in rhythm with the leader. The person with that number then must call out another. If a player fails to call out a number or does it out of rhythm, he must go to the end of the circle and take the lowest number. Everyone else moves up one place and advances one number.

Alphabet Rhythm. When number rhythm has been mastered, try alphabet rhythm. On the first snap you say a number, on the second a letter. The one who has the number you called must say a word beginning with that letter, then in perfect rhythm with the leader, call out a number on the next snap, and on the third snap a different letter. The player with that number must say a word beginning with that letter on the next snap, a number on the next, and a letter on the next and so on.

Remember: Slap, clap, snap, clap, 1-2-3-4. Practice a few times before you play the game to get everyone used to the rhythm.

Crazy Story

Give each family member an old magazine from which he is to cut out three pictures to paste on three pieces of construction paper, not letting other family members see his choice.

When all are finished, mix up the pictures and place them face down on the kitchen table. Dad or Mom start the "crazy story" by picking up a picture and beginning a story about it. Set the timer on the stove to go off after one minute, at which time the storyteller stops and the next person continues the story by picking up the second picture and using it to add something to the story already begun. Continue until all the pictures have been turned over and family members have each had three one-minute turns. You'll be surprised at the creativity and imagination of your children!

Easter Egg Hunt

Egg hunts are fun, even if bunnies and Easter eggs are not related to the true meaning of the resurrection day. Hide them indoors or outdoors depending on the weather.

Rake Yard

Raking the yard can be a fun family time if Mom and Dad work along with the children and follow the time outdoors with an interesting devotional time and a special treat.

Let's Read Together

Have you experienced the joys of reading aloud to your children? We did a lot of that when our boys were small, and they often mention how they loved it. Choose a book that will keep their interest. We read the Danny Orlis and Sugar Creek Gang series, but there are many other good ones from which to choose. Don't forget the classics, such as *Heidi, Swiss Family Robinson, Black Beauty, House at Pooh Corner.*

You may want to read short stories that can be finished in one evening. Anthologies are available at many Christian bookstores and libraries. Sunday school papers have good short stories, too.

SOURCES

Clint Bonner, *A Hymn Is Born* (Chicago: Wilcox and Follet Co., 1952).

F.W. Boreham, *A Temple of Topaz* (Philadelphia: Judson Press, 1928).

George Douglas, *American Book of Days* (New York: H.W. Wilson Co., 1937).

Lynne Martin, *Peacocks* (New York: William Morrow Co., 1975).

Flannery O'Conner, *Mystery and Manners* (New York: Farrar, Straus and Giroux, 1961).

5

May

It is believed that the fifth month of our calendar year was named after the ancient Roman earth goddess Maia to whom the month was dedicated.

One of May's best known holidays is Mother's Day, which always falls on the second Sunday of the month. Long ago the Romans had a spring festival dedicated to Cybele, the mother of gods. The English observed a "Mothering Sunday" half way through Lent. Our modern Mother's Day did not become an official holiday until 1914.

Anna M. Jarvis spent six or seven years making visits and writing letters to influential persons in order to establish Mother's Day in our country. Finally President Woodrow Wilson proclaimed the second Sunday in May as Mother's Day. A number of other countries, including Afghanistan, India, Spain, and Costa Rica also established a day especially for mothers.

Memorial Day is the other important holiday in May. That holiday, which now falls on the last Monday of the month, was originally established to honor the soldiers, both Confederate and Union, who died in the Civil War. Today we honor the dead of all wars and also put flowers on the graves of relatives and friends on Memorial or Decoration Day.

May is a busy month with Mother's Day teas, graduations, and other events to wind up the school year. It is a month to think about those who have sacrificed for us: the mothers that gave us birth, and the brave men who fought and died to defend our freedom.

ESPECIALLY FOR PARENTS

Children need more than food, clothing, shelter, and money for a college education—they need love.

Even dogs suffer from lack of attention and love. An official in the King County Humane Society shelter in Seattle stated, "Unless petted regularly, pooches in pounds lose their self-esteem and self-destruct." Playful, gamboling dogs gradually turn into fearful, unhappy, cringing animals when unnoticed and unloved. To prevent this, officials of the shelter have launched a program called Pet Therapy. Animal lovers volunteer to pet, cuddle, and walk the dogs in order to keep them happy and healthy.

If dogs go into emotional depression when deprived of love, how much more will humans? In our busy, hectic world, do we find time to say "I love you" to the people we love?

The bumper sticker asks, "Have you hugged your kid today?" Everybody needs a hug once in a while, even our adolescent and grownup chidren. They need reassurance of our love more than we realize.

Bright Valley of Love, by Edna Hong, is the story of a boy named Gunther, living in Nazi Germany. Given up by his parents, he was grudgingly cared for by his grandmother, who kept him locked up in a bedroom all day while she worked. Her only words to the boy were scoldings. Over and over again she told him, "You are nothing but a nothing!"

At six years of age Gunther could neither walk nor talk. Finally the father and grandmother, certain the boy was hopelessly retarded, took him to a home for handicapped children where a doctor diagnosed his problem as "the worst case of rickets I have ever seen."

Gunther slowly began to respond to the treatment he received from the kind workers at this home. Good food, sunshine, and love changed Gunther into a normal boy who eventually learned to talk, read, sing, and walk. It was love that changed him the most.

Love can change our children, too, but it must be expressed. Fathers often find this harder to do than mothers. Many children long for their fathers' expression of love. Some who do not receive love from their fathers have difficulty in later life believing in a heavenly Father's love.

Dad, you represent the heavenly Father to your children. As they respond to you, they will learn to respond to Him.

We need to verbalize our love often. Words, however, are empty unless backed by deeds. We can *show* our love to our children and mates in many different ways. Our boys mentioned after they were grown how much it meant to them to know that each evening after school there would be a hot meal waiting for them at home. Even though the fare was simple (they learned to love hash), it was wholesome, hot, and tasty. It told them they were loved and cared for.

My husband, though a busy pastor, showed his love by attending, whenever possible, athletic functions in which our sons were involved. He followed their activities with interest and support.

Even discipline is a way of showing love when administered fairly and with concern.

Along with love comes understanding. As parents we should try to understand our children by recalling our own childhood and adolescent experiences. Too often we expect our children to look at matters the way we do now after years of experience, instead of remembering how we felt about those things when we were their age.

Our children ask for our love in many ways. They want and need our love more than anything else we can give them. Express your love to your child today.

FAMILY DEVOTIONS

BIBLE STUDY: BIBLE TOWN

Make a Bible town to teach your children the books of the Old and New Testaments. Your part is to draw the streets; their part is to cut out houses from construction paper, label them with the names of the books, and paste them on the proper street. This is a project that could be continued all month. By the end of that time your children should know the books of the Bible.

Names of streets for the Old Testament:

Moses Avenue
History Drive
Poetry Lane
Major Prophets Boulevard
Minor Prophets Street

Names of streets for the New Testament:

Gospel Lane
History Boulevard
Pauline Epistles Avenue
General Epistles Drive
Prophecy Street

To make simple houses out of construction paper, cut strips 2 inches by 6 inches and fold into thirds. Fold the edges of the two outside thirds under for pasting. Print the name of the Bible book on the middle third. Glue or tape the "house" on the proper street. The streets can be drawn on a large piece of poster board.

As you work on your Bible town, talk about how the Bible was written. Although God used men to write the words of the Bible, He told them what to write. He used many different kinds of men, from prophets and fishermen to farmers and doctors. Although they all wrote at different times and in different places, their message is the same, because it is God's message. God tells us through the writers what He is like and what we are like. He tells us of His great plan to send His Son to die for our sins. He tells us how we can be saved by faith in His Son. God tells us in the Bible how to live. If we obey this Book we will be happy and successful in God's sight. God also tells us how to die. The Bible tells us about life after death and how we can go to the wonderful place called heaven when we die if we trust in Jesus to save us.

There is no other book in all the world like the Bible. Jesus said, "Heaven and earth will pass away, but My words shall not pass away" (Matthew 24:35).

Bible Drill

Give Bibles to each family member and have a contest to see who can find the assigned verses the fastest.

Start with verses in the first book, Genesis, the last book, Revelation, and the middle book, Psalms. Be sure to have the finder read his verse aloud. Explain the meaning of the verse if he does not understand it. Here are some good verses to start with:

Genesis 1:1   Psalm 47:6
Revelation 3:20   Genesis 8:22

Psalm 27:1	Revelation 21:4
Genesis 1:27	Psalm 46:1
Psalm 121:2	Genesis 50:20
Revelation 15:3	Psalm 147:5
Psalm 23:6	Revelation 22:20

After your children have become proficient in finding verses in these three books, try a Bible drill in several other books. Give one point for finding the verse first, another for telling what Bible street it's on.

Children love this kind of competition and learn as they play. If you have an only child, or only one old enough to compete, use an egg timer to see if he can find a verse in a given number of minutes, or have the child compete with you.

More verses for Bible drills:

Exodus 20:8	Luke 9:24
Leviticus 19:18	Hebrews 13:1
John 1:12	Numbers 32:23
Jeremiah 31:3	James 1:2
Exodus 19:5	Luke 15:10
Proverbs 3:5-6	1 John 4:10
Isaiah 53:6	1 Peter 5:7
Hosea 14:1	Matthew 6:44

Memory Verse: "Heaven and earth will pass away, but My words shall not pass away" (Matthew 24:35).

Tiny Tot Verse: "My words shall not pass away" (Matthew 24:35).

A HERO TO FOLLOW: RANSOMED AT LAST

Kaboo shook with fear when he saw his tormentor coming towards him with the whip.* Obediently he lay down to endure his daily beating. Once, twice, three times the heavy vine whip came down on the boy's back. Four, five, six lashes! Then Kaboo lost count. Before the beating was over he was nearly unconscious.

After a time Kaboo realized that his tormentor had left him. Cautiously he raised his head and looked around. Not far away his captors

* Adapted from *Christian Youth*, American Sunday School Union. Used by permission.

were having a drunken feast. Eagerly they reached for a large jug that held intoxicating liquor.

Kaboo fell back and lay very still. Perhaps if he did not move they would forget that he was there. A helpless sigh escaped his lips.

His father was a chieftain of the Kru people, and he a prince. When the Krus had been defeated in a tribal war, Kaboo was forced to become a slave of the conquerors until the ransom was paid. But the Kru tribe could not satisfy the demands of the conquering chief. They were too poor to redeem their prince, Kaboo. The conquering tribe was cruel, anyway; no matter how much his father offered, it was never enough. Kaboo would be a slave forever.

Or would his enemies kill him? Kaboo shuddered as he remembered the terrible deaths some of their captives had suffered. But perhaps even such a death would be better than the living death he was experiencing. How could he continue to endure the merciless beatings?

The drunken men began to shout and dance. Kaboo's heart beat fast with fear. What would they do to him next?

Cautiously the captive boy turned his head to look. Nobody seemed to notice him. If only he could escape to the nearby woods. But such a hope was foolish. Suddenly Kaboo heard a voice say, "Flee to the forest." Noiselessly he sprang to his feet. A new strength surged into his emaciated body as he ran swiftly. He had not gone far when the drunken men noticed his absence. Enraged, they grasped their weapons and ran in pursuit.

Kaboo could hear them coming so he ran faster. They were drunk, and he was filled with a strange strength that gave wings to his feet.

At last the kidnapped prince found a hollow tree in which to hide. His pursuers searched for him in vain and finally turned back. The African boy waited until darkness fell before continuing his journey. Danger lurked in the jungle at night, but Kaboo preferred those dangers to the risk of meeting enemies by day. So he traveled in the darkness, finding roots and berries to eat, and hid by day.

After days of tramping through the forest, the young prince finally found a foreign settlement. Was it a slave colony? Cautiously he drew near and found to his joy that it was a slave-liberating colony.

Kaboo obtained work on a coffee plantation. There he met a boy from his own tribe who was a Christian and persuaded Kaboo to go with him to church. At first Kaboo did not understand the teaching of the Bible, but gradually the light began to dawn in his heart.

The missionary explained to Kaboo that One had come from heaven to be a ransom for men's sins. He too had been treated cruelly, beaten, mocked, and at last put to death. By His death He had paid the price for man's sins and purchased for them forgiveness and eternal life.

Kaboo learned that Jesus Christ, the Son of God, was the One who had done this for him. The African boy remembered the voice that had urged him to flee from his tormentors. He recalled the strength he had received from an unknown source. He marveled at his safe journey through the dangerous forest. Surely even before Kaboo knew Him, God had been leading him.

His father had not been able to ransom him from his captors, but Jesus Christ had paid enough to ransom him from the captivity of a greater enemy, sin and evil.

Humbly Kaboo bowed and received Jesus Christ as his substitute and Savior. Upon receiving baptism, Kaboo took a new name, Samuel Morris. He studied the Bible under the direction of the missionary. Later he made his way to the coast. There Sammy persuaded a sea captain to hire him as a cabin boy. After a miserable trip during which the crew members tormented the black boy, Sammy arrived in America.

Even though Sammy was uneducated by American standards, he loved Jesus very much. American Christians sometimes felt ashamed when they saw that Sammy loved his Lord more than they did. They listened to him, and many came to Jesus. Many more were challenged to live for Jesus.

Sammy studied at Taylor University in Indiana, planning to return to Africa to help his people. But God had other plans. He chose to take Sammy to heaven before he could return to his homeland. But Sammy's life and testimony had not been in vain. Many of his fellow classmates from the university were inspired by his life and testimony and gave their lives to carry on God's work in Sammy's homeland as well as in other countries.

Questions for Thought:

1. Why was Kaboo a captive?
2. Who helped him escape from his enemies and find friends?
3. What great thing happened to him at the slave-liberating colony?
4. What name did he choose at his baptism?
5. How did God use Sammy in America?
6. How can God use you?

Memory Verse: "But God demonstrates His own love toward us, in that while we were yet sinners, Christ died for us" (Romans 5:8).

Tiny Tot Verse: "Christ died for us" (Romans 5:8).

NATURE CORNER: COURAGEOUS SUSIE

Susie Salmon hatches from an egg in the gravel of a small stream. She spends her first days darting about eating insects and hiding from danger.

After she has grown to be about five inches long, she and her brothers and sisters leave the quiet stream where they were born. They set off for the mysterious ocean and an exciting adventure.

Dangers lurk along the way. Hungry bears are good at scooping up fish from a shallow place. Birds looking for food are ready to swoop down. It takes three months before Susie and her brothers and sisters reach the Pacific Ocean. Except for the danger from enemies, it is an easy trip because they are swimming downstream with the current.

How exciting to reach the vast ocean at last. So much room to swim and explore. Such a variety of food to eat. But Susie must be careful—larger fish and seals would like to eat her for dinner.

As Susie swims and eats, she grows into a fine adult salmon. After four years of ocean living, she suddenly longs to go back to the little stream where she was born.

The trip back to the little stream is much more difficult than the one to the ocean. By now Susie is a fisherman's prize. She has to avoid fish hooks and fish nets all the way. She also has to swim upstream against the current.

Susie sometimes has to leap over rocks and waterfalls that are in her way, but she is a good jumper—she can leap as high as four times her own length.

When Susie reaches a man-made dam she stops in bewilderment. How can she get over the rushing water? Not willing to give up, Susie finds little pools going up the side of the dam called a fish ladder. Susie leaps from pool to pool until she is finally over the top and on her way again.

Susie finally reaches the little stream where she was born. She lays her eggs in the sand, using her tail to cover them with sand. The eggs will not hatch until spring. By that time Susie will be through with her short life.

Isn't Susie a courageous fish? She doesn't give up even when it's hard. She swims against the current and even leaps over obstacles to reach her destination.

Sometimes boys and girls have to swim upstream, too. Maybe your friends are swimming downstream, doing what is easy but wrong. Sometimes it is very hard to be different from those around you, to do the right things when others are doing wrong.

Did you know that Susie's creator gives her courage to do what she does? He will give you courage, too. He has promised to never leave or forsake us.

Think about ways you are "swimming upstream" at school and play. Discuss real life situations. Read the following verses to see how God will help you:

Matthew 28:20
1 Corinthians 10:13
Philippians 4:13, 19
Hebrews 14:5-6

Memory Verse: "I can do all things through Him who strengthens me" (Philippians 4:13).

Tiny Tot Verse: "Be not afraid" (Matthew 14:27).

HYMN STORY: "I MUST TELL JESUS"

Elisha Hoffman was a pastor who lived over fifty years ago. He was lonely because his wife died when she was only thirty-two years old, but instead of feeling sorry for himself, Mr. Hoffman worked to comfort other sorrowing people.

One day as he was visiting the people of his church, he came to the home of a woman who was in such trouble she wrung her hands and cried, "Brother Hoffman, what shall I do?"

The kind pastor said, "You cannot do better than take all your sorrows to Jesus. You must tell Jesus."

"Yes," agreed the woman, "I must tell Jesus." She did and was comforted.

When the pastor returned to his home he sat down and wrote the words of this hymn. As you sing it, think of what you would like to tell

Jesus. You can tell Him both your joys and sorrows; there is nothing that you cannot talk to Him about.

I Must Tell Jesus

I must tell Jesus all of my trials;
I cannot bear these burdens alone;
In my distress He kindly will help me;
He ever loves and cares for His own.

Chorus
I must tell Jesus! I must tell Jesus!
I cannot bear my burdens alone;
I must tell Jesus! I must tell Jesus!
Jesus can help me, Jesus alone.

I must tell Jesus all of my troubles;
He is a kind, compassionate Friend;
If I but ask Him, He will deliver,
Make of my troubles quickly an end.

O how the world to evil allures me!
O how my heart is tempted to sin!
I must tell Jesus, and He will help me
Over the world the victory to win.

Discuss the things you can talk to Jesus about. Pray together about those things.

Memory Verse: "I love the Lord, because He hears my voice and my supplications. Because He has inclined His ear to me, therefore I shall call upon Him as long as I live" (Psalm 116:1).

Tiny Tot Verse: "He hears my voice" (Psalm 116:1).

ACTIVITIES

Make May Baskets
Woven May Basket. Cut one color of construction paper into 1-inch strips, each 8 inches long. Cut another color into a square 8 inches by 8 inches. Fold the square in half and cut 1-inch strips from the folded side to within one inch of the edge.
Open up. Weave the strips of contrasting color through the open-

ings, alternating to give a woven effect. When finished, put corners together to form a triangular May basket. Glue or staple on a handle.

Oblong May Basket. Take a piece of colored construction paper. Measure and draw lines two inches from each end and on sides. Cut on each corner. Fold up ends and sides to make a basket. Paste together or tape. Paste on a handle. Paste pretty pictures on the sides cut from old greeting cards.

Fill your baskets with spring flowers and a few wrapped candies or cookies to give to a favorite friend. These are especially appropriate for elderly and shut-in friends.

Mother's Day Gifts

Dad should arrange for a family night without Mom. Send her to visit Grandma or a friend. While she is gone he could take the children shopping to pick out inexpensive gifts for Mom. Wrap them in colorful paper and hide until Mother's Day.

Make Mother's Day cards out of pieces of construction paper and old greeting cards. Print as many reasons as you can under the line "Why My Mother Is the Best" or write an original poem to Mother.

Hopscotch

Hopscotch has been a favorite springtime game for years in countries all over the world.

Up to four can play. Each player has a small piece of wood or a pebble which they put in square 1. The first player hops over square 1 on one foot and into square 2, still on one foot. He can put both feet down on 4 and 5 and 7 and 8. When he reaches 7 and 8 he must make a jumping turn around so his feet land in 7 and 8 only facing the other way. He then makes his return to square 2 where he must pick up his piece of wood while standing on one foot, and hop over square 1 to the starting place. He then throws his piece of wood into square 2 and the next player takes a turn. The second player must do the same as the first except now there are 2 squares where he cannot step. If a player steps in a square where someone's block is or steps on a line he must return to the starting place and wait for another turn. The player who succeeds in getting his block in each square: 1, 2, 3, 4, 5, 6, 7, 8, and back down again, 7, 6, 5, 4, 3, 2, 1 returning to the starting point, is the winner.

Hopscotch squares can be drawn on the sidewalk or driveway with chalk or scratched in firm dirt with a stick.

Jumping Rope

Jumping rope is another springtime activity. It is even good for Mom and Dad to try. At least they can watch and cheer when their child skips one hundred times without missing.

Dad and Mom can get on each end of the rope too and let the children jump. Try High Water, turning the rope about 8 inches from the ground, and Hot Pepper, turning it as fast as possible.

Go to the Park

Most city parks have playground equipment which children enjoy. It's extra special when Dad pushes the swings or Mom gets on one end of the teeter-totter.

Plant a Garden

Children will learn important lessons as they plant seeds and watch them grow with you. Let them have small garden plots of their own. Talk about the miracle of life as you plant the tiny seeds that will one day be green plants and vegetables.

Bird Watching

Bird watching is fun, especially if you keep a notebook listing the various kinds you see. List their size, colors, markings, special features, song or call, and actions.

Get books from the library to help you identify the various birds. Talk about their eating, mating, and nesting habits. Make birdhouses for your backyard. Make a feeder for hummingbirds by wiring a pill bottle to a bush. Add water mixed with red food color and sugar. Hummingbirds love the color red and will go after the sugar water eagerly with their long beaks.

Early morning is the best time for bird-watching hikes. Go to city parks if you cannot get to a rural wooded area. Wear drab-colored clothes to remain unnoticed. You can also watch birds in your own backyard.

Paste pictures of different birds on flashcards and learn to identify them all.

Baseball Games or Track Meets

If Bobby or Susie are on baseball or track teams, the whole family should attend the events and cheer them on. Win or lose, a special treat afterwards at the ice-cream shop is great. Take the whole family to see a major league game once in a while, complete with hot dogs, popcorn, and peanuts.

SOURCES

American Book of Days (New York: Bobley Publishing Corp., 1979).

Ernest K. Emurian, *Hymn Stories for Programs* (Grand Rapids: Baker Book House, 1963).

George S. Fichter, *Fishes* (New York: Golden Press, 1963).

Edna Hong, *Bright Valley of Love* (Minneapolis: Augsburg Press, 1976).

F.D. Ommaney, *The Fishes* (New York: Time, Inc., 1967).

"Petting Therapy Is Saving Pooches" (Everett *Herald,* December 31, 1980).

6

June

June is a magic month. School is over for the year, summer begins, families start taking vacations; young couples get married.

The sixth month of our present calendar may have been named after Juno, the Roman goddess of women and children. Now June has become a favorite month for weddings.

Some countries hold special celebrations on June 21 to welcome the beginning of summer. In Austria it is considered lucky for couples to leap over bonfires hand in hand on this longest day of the year. For people in the southern hemisphere, June is a winter month. They build bonfires to call back the spring.

In the United States, June is National Rose Month, Dairy Month, National Ragweed Control Month, and the month in which we celebrate Father's Day.

For families it is the beginning of a three-month vacation from school. Don't anticipate those months with dread, wondering how you can cope with having your kids home every day. Instead, look upon it as three months of opportunity to teach, train, and play with them, molding their lives. They grow up so quickly—don't lose your opportunity!

ESPECIALLY FOR PARENTS

Most parents are concerned when Bobby has a stomach ache and take measures to bring him relief. But are we equally concerned about the *mental* health of our children? What about low self-esteem, moodiness, irritability, aggressive behavior, listlessness, boredom? Are we alert to those symptoms? Do we make an effort to get to the bottom of them or write them off as part of our child's unchangeable temperament?

Parents' Attitudes Are Important

Children catch the attitudes of their parents at home more quickly than they catch measles at school. Does Dad growl and mutter about conditions at work or the way the country is going? Does Mom complain and sigh a lot? Children will soon be growling, complaining, and sighing too.

My three-year-old granddaughter said with a sigh to her doll one evening, "I've had a hard day!" Where do you suppose she learned that? Probably from her grandmother!

Look around at families you know. You will notice that inevitably the children's attitudes reflect those of their parents or others close to them. Look at your own children and see if you have passed negative attitudes on to them.

Some of the greatest gifts you can give your children are the positive attitudes of optimism, gratitude, and faith that foster good mental health.

Encourage Self-Esteem

George developed a mammoth inferiority complex because his older brother constantly put him down. Even though he was a good-looking man and an expert in his field of work, he had no self-esteem. To escape from the self he didn't like, he began to drink excessively and destroy his mind and body. That is what an extreme inferiority complex can do. Even a lesser case of inferiority can result in myriad problems and sufferings.

All of us have areas in which we feel inadequate. Most of us would change certain things about ourselves if we could. But some things cannot be changed—they must be accepted.

In some cultures, parents say only derogatory things about their children in an effort to make them undesirable to evil spirits who would capture them. We would never adopt such a pagan idea, yet many parents are reluctant to praise their children. How often do we point out the things they do wrong? How seldom do we praise them for the things they do right? How often do parents compare one child with another, nag, criticize, destroy self-esteem? Instead, think of ways to build up your child's self-esteem, his confidence. Self-esteem is essential to good mental health.

Turn Off the Tube

There are some good programs on television through which our children can learn about other cultures, space travel, new discoveries, exotic animals, history, and other useful information. We must take extreme caution, however, that at the same time they do not learn wrong attitudes towards God and moral behavior.

Busy parents may sit their children in front of a television set just to get some peace and quiet without realizing the damage some TV programs can do a child's mental and spiritual health. Even cartoons that seem harmless often portray violence and aggressive behavior. Catchy commercials can influence your children toward secularism, materialism, and humanism.

Even if television did none of those things to your child, it could still be harmful by stifling creativity, making a child a passive spectator instead of a participant. It dulls his capacity to entertain himself and find enjoyment in common things. If you want him to maintain good mental health, be careful how much television your child watches.

Spark Creativity

Television wasn't in common use when I was a child. I had a glorious childhood without it. My sisters, brother, and I found plenty to amuse ourselves with when our chores were finished. We swung from branch to branch in the vine maples, slid down a grassy hill in gunny sacks, floated pieces of wood down our stream, made up plays and performed them for each other, wrote poems, climbed trees, gave life to our dolls, and read books. I can't remember ever being bored.

Even if you don't have vine maples, climbable trees, and a stream, you can spark your child's creativity by providing him with materials to make things: construction paper, glue, felt-tipped pens, old greeting cards, scraps of cloth, needles, thread, pieces of wood, tools, old magazines and catalogs.

A friend of mine tells how her mother supplied her and her siblings with small blocks of wood left over from their father's carpentry work. They pasted pictures from catalogs on the pieces to make delightful furniture for rooms contructed from cardboard boxes.

Big cardboard boxes (the kind refrigerators and stoves come in) make excellent houses out in the backyard, often big enough for several children. Tree houses are oodles of fun, especially when Dad helps to make them safe and sturdy. Old blankets over chairs or tables make passable indoor tents to provide hours of fun for children on rainy summer afternoons.

I pity the child who has every toy and game available. Give him a board, paints, and some old buttons, and let him figure out a game of his own. He'll be so proud when he has created his own original invention!

Be a Family That Reads

A warm June afternoon is a good time to take your children to the public library. Show them where they can find good storybooks—books about famous people, foreign countries, interesting projects.

Take time each day this month to read to your children a book you can all enjoy. Try a classic such as *Heidi, Swiss Family Robinson,* or *The Yearling.* Then read a Christian classic such as *The Tanglewoods' Secret, Little Pilgrim's Progress,* or one of the books in the Danny Orlis series. You will be nurturing your child's mental health by feeding his mind with noble thoughts and aspirations.

One of the highlights of our family vacation when our boys were between the ages of eight and twelve was a trip to a fascinating second-hand bookstore in Minneapolis. We spent time browsing through the books, and each of us selected several to buy. There wasn't much noise in the car for several hours after that stop—each of us was absorbed in one of our new books. Sometimes we have visited libraries, too, during our vacation trips, especially if it rained and we couldn't be outdoors. Our boys loved spending a few hours in a library.

FAMILY DEVOTIONS

BIBLE STUDY: TRUTH VERSUS LIES

Teach your children to tell themselves the truth from God's Word. Explain that when we become unhappy and discouraged we are listening to Satan's lies instead of to God. Encourage them to read and memorize God's truth.

Let them help by making a list of lies we tell ourselves. Refute those lies with appropriate Bible passages. Here are some samples—you will think of more:

Lie	Bible Passage
I can't	Philippians 4:13
I'm afraid	Isaiah 43:1
I'm unhappy because I can't have something I want	Hebrews 13:5
Nobody likes me	Jeremiah 31:3
Everyone is against me	Romans 8:13
I'm not good-looking	1 Samuel 16:7
I wish I looked different	Romans 9:20-21

Bible characters who told themselves lies:

Jacob. When Jacob's sons came back from Egypt where they had gone to buy food, they told Jacob they could not go back to buy more food unless they took Benjamin, the youngest brother, with them. Jacob said, "All these things are against me" (Genesis 42:36). Read Genesis 46:29-31 and 48:11 to show that Jacob was telling himself a lie. Then read Romans 8:31.

Job. Job lost his cattle, sheep, donkeys, and children, and then his health (he became afflicted with boils). He said, "My eye will not again see good" (Job 7:7). Read Job 42:10-17 to show that he was wrong. Then read Romans 8:28.

Naomi. Naomi was sad because her husband and two sons had died in the land of Moab. She came back to her hometown, Bethlehem, with her daughter-in-law, Ruth. She said, "The Almighty has dealt very bitterly with me" (Ruth 1:20). Read Ruth 2-4 to see how God took care of her and made her happy in the end. Then read Jeremiah 29:11. (If your children are small, tell the story from the Bible in simple words rather than reading it.)

Ask your children what they learned from these Bible stories. Pray together that you will always tell the truth instead of listening to Satan's lies.

Memory Verse: "For I know the plans that I have for you, declared the Lord, plans for welfare and not for calamity to give you a future and a hope" (Jeremiah 29:11).

Tiny Tot Verse: "The Lord is good" (Nahum 1:7).

A HEROINE TO FOLLOW: A BEAUTIFUL PLAN

Do you ever feel ugly? Jane did.* In fact, she was so ashamed of the way she looked she avoided her handsome father when they were at gatherings together, thinking he would be embarrassed to have her as his daughter. Because of a curvature of the spine, Jane's back was crooked, her head tilted to one side, and she walked with a pigeon-toed shuffle.

Because of the way she felt about her physical deformity, Jane's heart went out to others suffering with handicaps. Eventually surgery corrected her deformity, but she never forgot how rejected she had felt when odd and ugly. Because of this, she dedicated her life to helping people who were handicapped by disease, poverty, or ignorance.

The girl who suffered from being deformed when she was young was none other than Jane Addams. Together with a friend she opened and operated Hull House in the slums in the late 1800s and became one of America's first social workers. She was more than a social worker and social reformer—the *New York Times* called her "The American people's most understanding and compassionate friend."

Nobody knows how many slum dwellers were lifted from their unsanitary, hopeless condition through the efforts of that compassionate woman. Today we are still benefiting from the social reforms she began. Would Jane Addams have felt such compassion if she had never experienced those feelings of inferiority because of her handicap? Would she have given her life for the suffering if she had never suffered herself?

God is sovereign over all. He decides what we will look like, what abilities and handicaps we will have, what home we will be born into. The Bible tells us He is no respecter of persons, which means He doesn't have favorites. Sometimes it seems as if He does, but that is because we can see only one side of the picture.

The Lord prepared Jane Addams for her lifework by permitting her to be deformed and ugly. But look how beautifully things turned out in the end, not only for her but for the hundreds of people she helped.

God has a beautiful plan for you, too. He may have to allow something unpleasant to come to you in order to work out His plan. If you permit Him to work and lead, if you praise and trust Him instead of

* Adapted from *My Delight*, Union Gospel Press. Used by permission.

grumbling, the end result will be beautiful for you too and for the many you will influence.

Discuss things about your children that they wish were different: looks, size, abilities, etc. Talk about God's wisdom in making those things as they are.

Memory Verse: "How precious also are thy thoughts unto me, O God! How great is the sum of them! If I should count them, they are more in number than the sand" (Psalm 139:17-18).

Tiny Tot Verse: "The Lord is my shepherd" (Psalm 23:1).

NATURE CORNER: THE BUG WHO WINS THE POPULARITY CONTEST

Did you know that there is a bug named after Mary, the mother of Jesus? The bright-colored ladybug is the insect that was so honored years ago by the people of Europe. They loved ladybugs because they ate the aphids, scale insects, and mites that threatened to destroy their crops.

When the growing season was over, the people of Europe burned their hop vines to get rid of aphid eggs. They didn't want to burn their ladybug friends, so they made up the little poem we know so well: "Ladybug, Ladybug, fly away home; Your house is on fire and your children will burn."

Many insects, such as flies and mosquitoes, are pests and spread disease. Other insects eat the leaves of garden plants or destroy whole fields. We try to kill them by swatting or spraying. But ladybugs are helpful insects, so nobody wants to destroy them.

Some people actually collect them to sell. When the ladybugs are hibernating they are collected and put into refrigeration until spring. Then they are packed in straw and sold to farmers and gardeners who release them into their fields and gardens to eat insects harmful to the crops. One year some ladybugs from Australia helped save thousands of oranges in California by eating the cottony cushion scales that had attacked the crop.

Why is the ladybug such a popular insect? Because she's not a pest, she's a helper.

If you're like the ladybug, people will want you around, too. There are many ways you can be a helper at home and at school.

Ladybugs don't really know they're helpers—they simply like to eat aphids and other pests. But you can plan ways to be helpful, not just to be popular, but because you love Jesus and want to please Him. Being a helper is one way to serve Him.

Questions for Thought:

1. Why do people swat and spray mosquitoes and flies?
2. Why is the ladybug popular?
3. How can you be like the ladybug? Think of three ways.
4. What does Jesus think of our being helpful?

Memory Verse: "And whatever you do in word or deed, do all in the name of the Lord Jesus, giving thanks through Him to God the Father" (Colossians 3:17).

Tiny Tot: "Do all in the name of the Lord Jesus" (Colossians 3:17).

HYMN STORY: "GOD WILL TAKE CARE OF YOU"

J.C. Penney had been a wealthy man. He had stores all across the nation. But hard times came. Nearly everyone lost their money, including Mr. Penney. How could he pay his debts? How could he go on?

Mr. Penney became sick from worry. He was in a hospital and wanted to die. Early one morning Mr. Penney felt an urge to get out of his hospital bed and walk down the corridor. He came upon a group of people having early morning devotions. They were singing, "God Will Take Care of You."

God spoke to Mr. Penney through that hymn. He realized that all was not lost after all. God would take care of him and help him start over.

As Mr. Penney stopped worrying and began trusting God, his health returned. He was able to leave the hospital and start working. God blessed him, and he became successful again.

When you see a J.C. Penney store, think of this song that inspired and helped Mr. Penney when he felt hopeless and afraid. Sing it when you feel afraid and are ready to give up. Then give thanks for God's care and protection.

God Will Take Care of You

Be not dismayed what e'er betide,
  God will take care of you.
Beneath His wings of love abide,
  God will take care of you.

Chorus
God will take care of you,
  Through every day, O'er all the way;
He will take care of you,
  God will take care of you.

Through days of toil when heart doth fail
  God will take care of you;
When dangers fierce your path assail,
  God will take care of you.

All you may need He will provide,
  God will take care of you,
Nothing you ask will be denied,
  God will take care of you.

W.S. Martin

Memory Verse: "The Lord is my light and my salvation; Whom shall I fear? The Lord is the defense of my life; Whom shall I dread?" (Psalm 27:1).

Tiny Tot Verse: "The Lord is my light" (Psalm 27:1).

ACTIVITIES

Ant Farm
The writer of Proverbs tells us to go to the ant and be wise. Your children will learn a great deal from observing ants at work. Sometimes you can observe them in their natural habitat, scurrying around and carrying food home to their nests. If this is not feasible, why not buy your children an ant farm at a toy shop? The farms are under ten dollars and come complete with sand and little farm buildings. They are enclosed in glass so the ants can be seen at work from either side. You can order the ants by mail and receive with them directions for feeding.

You and your children will be fascinated as you watch the ants build tunnels in the sand, dispose of their dead, store their food, and do many other things.

Watching a tiny ant try repeatedly to pull a dead fly many times its size over an obstruction in the ant farm taught me perseverance. Their busyness teaches industriousness.

There are many books on ants written for children that can be borrowed at your local library. Your children will want to learn all they can about these fascinating insects.

An ant farm is an ideal gift for a child who lives in an apartment where pets aren't allowed or for one who is allergic to animal hair.

Lemonade

Choose sides. Team One should decide on a vocation to represent and discuss how they will act it out. Then the two teams stand facing each other in lines about thirty feet apart and repeat the following dialogue:

> Team One (advancing about ten feet): Here we come.
> Team Two: Where from?
> Team One: New Orleans.
> Team Two: What's your trade?
> Team One: Lemonade.
> Team Two: Get to work!

Members of Team One then act out the vocation or activity they have chosen: driving a tractor, planting potatoes, caring for a baby, preaching a sermon, building a house.

Team Two guesses what they are doing. When they guess correctly, Team One must run back to their line while Team Two pursues them. Any person tagged must join Team Two. Then Team Two goes through the same procedure. The teams need not be more than two persons.

Animal Blindman's Bluff

Blindfold one player and furnish him with a long stick. He stands in the center of the circle the others form around him. The others dance around the circle until he hits the ground with his stick. Then they must stand still. He holds out the stick to a player telling him the name of an animal. The player must imitate the sound this animal makes. If the blindfolded player can guess who is making the sound, he exchanges places with him. If not, he must extend his stick to someone else and try again.

Stone, Paper, Scissors

This game is played in many countries. The Japanese use it as we would draw straws to determine who gets to be first in a game or receive other favors.

Two at a time play this game. Each holds out his fist in front of him. Each player strikes the top of a table or his knee three times. The third time he either keeps his fist clenched to represent a stone, opened out flat to represent paper, or with two fingers spread apart to represent scissors. If both players are the same, they try again. The winners are paper over stone (stone can be wrapped in paper), scissors over paper (scissors can cut paper), stone over scissors (stone can break scissors).

Visit a Family

One of the most delightful experiences of my childhood was when our family visited other families with children. Let the children help you decide who to visit and let them help you make some treats to take. Invite the friends back to share one of your family evenings.

Feed the Ducks

Do you live near a lake? Take stale bread with you and let your children feed the birds and ducks. It's a beautiful way to spend a summer evening together. You could have your devotions right out by the water, sitting on your blanket. You might want to stop for ice-cream cones on the way home.

Follow the Leader

Choose a leader and follow him in whatever antics he thinks up. If he jumps, the followers must jump. If he hops, the followers must too. This can be played indoors as well as outdoors if your house is large enough.

Hunt for Treasure

Do you need help cleaning your attic or garage? Has junk accumulated in the children's bedrooms? Make cleanup day fun by enlisting everyone in a treasure hunt. Look for items that can be sold for profit. Arrange the treasures on a table and have a yard sale. Proceeds can go to a missionary project or for a family treat. Junk can go in big plastic bags to be taken to the dump. Returnable articles, such as bottles, can be returned to the store by the children.

Treasure Hike

Stop to collect aluminum cans that have been thrown from cars as you drive down the road. This will serve two purposes: it will make the countryside more beautiful and provide a little spending money for your children when you turn in the cans.

Berry Picking

If you live in an area where berries are available, go berry picking as a family. Taking a picnic lunch along with you will make the event special. Children can help prepare the berries for canning and freezing when you get home.

A Gift for Dad

Glue dried beans over the entire surface of a jar. It will make a pretty pen and pencil holder for Dad's desk. Or make an attractive plaque by gluing alphabet macaroni on a smooth board to read, "The World's Greatest Dad." Brush or spray on varnish and attach a hook for hanging. For an extra touch add a snapshot of yourself with Dad.

SOURCES

Deluxe Personal Appointment Book (New York: Bobley Publishing Corp., 1980).

Ada and Frank Graham, *The Milkweed and Its World of Animals* (New York: Doubleday and Co., 1976).

H.V. Harper, *Profiles of Protestant Saints* (New York: Fleet Press Corp., 1968).

Beatrice Plumb, *The Merchant Prince* (Grand Rapids: Baker Book House, n.d.).

7

July

According to the earliest Roman calendar, July was the fifth month of the year and simply called Quinctilis, the Latin word for fifth. When the calendar was reformed, Quinctilis became the seventh month, and its name was changed to *Julius* by the Roman Senate in honor of their dictator, Julius Caesar. In English Julius becomes July.

As a hot month July is a good time for vacations, swimming, camping, fishing, and other outdoor activities. It is also a good time to inspire patriotism in our children as we celebrate Independence Day. Don't let this important holiday digress to mere fun, feasting, and firecrackers. Talk about the courage and ideals of our forefathers. Sing patriotic songs with your children. Play the patriotic games listed in the activity section. Pledge allegiance to the flag. Talk about what it stands for. Discuss the four freedoms promised to us by the Bill of Rights: freedom of speech, of worship, from want, and from fear. Remind your family that very few people in the world enjoy the freedoms that we take for granted.

Talk about the government process. Who are your representatives, state senators, governor, mayor? Discuss the necessity for paying taxes to support schools, build roads, maintain parks, and sustain other public institutions.

Pray together for your country's leaders. Give thanks for the freedoms we enjoy in our United States of America.

ESPECIALLY FOR PARENTS

Vacationing with children can be more painful than pleasurable. How many parents heave a huge sigh of relief when they arrive home after a hectic vacation? On the other hand, vacations can be very special times of togetherness that you will always remember.

Preparation

Of course you will be frazzled, Mom, if you have to wash clothes, pack, make lunch, and clean up the house all on the morning you leave for a vacation. Plan ahead to avoid last minute tension.

Teach your children to pack their own suitcases. You'd be surprised how much this helps. Of course you'll have to make suggestions and give a quick check, but each child can do most of the work himself.

Assign jobs for each child to do the morning you leave. Susie will feel important preparing healthful snacks ahead of time: carrot and celery sticks, fruit, fruit juice, crackers and cheese. Let Bobby pack a small ice chest to keep these things cool.

Don't let Dad leave the oil changing until the morning you leave. Nothing is so frustrating to the family as to be all ready to go, only to find Dad in his greasy clothes tinkering under the hood of the car. For a smooth getaway, prepare the car a few days before you leave. Study the map, too, so that you know where you're going. It'll be much more enjoyable for everyone if you avoid last-minute delays.

Practice the Golden Rule

Once you are off, don't forget to "do unto others as you would have others do unto you." That goes for radio listening, open windows, airconditioning, and so on. This is a good opportunity to teach your children consideration of others.

We teach best by example. Don't listen to the radio all day or read and ignore the children. Think of fun things to do to make the time more enjoyable. (See Car Games in the activities section).

We took a trip from Iowa to Washington state one summer, going through the Black Hills and Yellowstone Park. The scenery was breathtaking! At the end of the trip we asked our three young boys what part of the trip they had enjoyed the most. They replied without hesitation: "The first night when we stopped at that amusement park to go on rides and play miniature golf."

That remark helped us to see things from the viewpoint of young boys. They enjoyed activity more than scenery, no matter how gorgeous the view was! After that we tried to keep this in mind on trips and take time to stop at parks and play games or at a lake for a swim. Even a game of Catch at a service station helped the boys get rid of some of their excess energy.

Involve Them

Let Bobby help read the map even if you have your course all planned. Let him add up the miles between cities so you'll know how far you have to go before lunch. You might let the children take turns deciding where you will stop to eat.

Assign one child to keep records, putting down mileage, cost of gas, meals, number of miles traveled in a day. You might encourage your children who can write to keep a daily journal of interesting things they see along the way.

Surprises

Why not prepare a surprise box for about four o'clock every afternoon when both parents and children are tired and tend to be irritable? Include such things as packages of sugarless gum, balloons to be blown up, toy cars, small books, games, any trinket that would amuse a child. They'll look forward all day to surprise time, and it will make that last hour or two before the evening meal tolerable. Maybe you'll even be able to read a bit.

Ideal Vacations for Families

Ideal vacations for families involve a minimum of traveling. When your tent or camper is set up for the week in an interesting spot, or when you have arrived at Grandma and Grandpa's, you have no further problem with boredom for either parents or children. For maximum vacation enjoyment, keep your traveling time to the minimum.

However, if you, like us, live miles away from loved ones and must make frequent trips across the country, take time to plan interesting activities that can be done in the car to give you an enjoyable time together.

Vacation at Home

Perhaps you are unable to take a vacation trip this year. Take day trips instead to parks, the beach, and other fun spots, returning home at night to eat dinner and sleep. If you like to camp but can't travel, just put up a tent and camp in the backyard.

FAMILY DEVOTIONS

BIBLE STUDY: WATCH YOUR WORDS!

The home is a refuge from the often cruel outside world. There family members can feel accepted, secure, and loved. What a pity when family members cut down one another and inflict serious wounds that take years to heal.

This Bible study is designed to help you teach your children what their words can do and encourage them to use words that support and build up family members and friends instead of words that discourage and destroy.

Find the following verses together and discuss them:

Proverbs 18:21. How can our tongues cause death? (They can kill hope, enthusiasm, self-confidence.) How can they bring life? (They can encourage, build up, strengthen.)

Proverbs 12:25. Can you think of some "good words" that would make a family member glad? ("I'm sorry." "The pancakes are great." "Thank you for ironing my shirt." "You look nice today." "You're getting better at making your bed." "I like that dress on you.")

Proverbs 12:18. How can we wound others by our words? Think of words that pierce like a sword. ("You're fat." "You're stupid." "Your hair looks awful." "You're always late." "You're a crybaby.")

Proverbs 10:19. Discuss the dangers of talking too much. (Others don't get a chance to express themselves. You are apt to bore others. You are apt to say things you shouldn't.)

Proverbs 29:20; James 1:19. What does it mean to be "hasty" in our words? (You talk first and think afterwards, say words in anger you later wish you could take back.)

Proverbs 27:2. Discuss bragging. (When are your words sharing, and when are they bragging? How much should you tell about your own achievements? What about the way in which you talk of them? Do you give credit to God for His help?)

Proverbs 17:9; 20:19. What about gossip, talking about the faults of others? (Ask yourself these three questions before you repeat gossip: Is it true? Is it kind? Is it necessary?)

Psalm 36:28; Ephesians 5:19-20. Why should we talk about the

Lord to one another? (It glorifies Him, encourages others and ourselves.) What happens when we give thanks? (It glorifies God, makes
people around us happy, makes us happy.)

Memory Verse: "Let the words of my mouth and the meditation
of my heart be acceptable in Thy sight, O Lord, my rock and my re-
deemer" (Psalm 19:14).

Tiny Tot Verse: "Speak truth" (Ephesians 4:25).

A HERO TO FOLLOW: BILLY THE CHAMPION

"Wake up, Billy." Mrs. Sunday shook the nine-year-old boy gently.*
"The cows are waiting for you."
Billy sat up and rubbed his eyes. It seemed like the middle of the
night. He pulled himself out of the warm covers, jumped into his
clothes, and started off for the farm where he milked ten cows every
morning.
Billy had worked hard since he was six years old to help his widowed
mother keep their family together. His father had died in the Civil
War, two months after Billy was born.
After the cows were milked, Billy hurried back to the two-room log
cabin for his breakfast. He knew it wouldn't be much, for his family
was extremely poor.
At the age of eleven Billy began to do men's work in the harvest
fields. The money he earned helped to keep starvation from the family.
On summer days when work was slack Billy climbed trees or looked
for eggs in the haystack. He often took his rifle to hunt for squirrels in
the woods or played baseball with the other boys in the neighborhood.
When Billy was twelve years old and his brother fourteen, his mother
could take care of them no longer. With a sad heart she sent them to an
orphanage for soldiers' children. Billy and his brother couldn't hold
back the tears when they left their mother at the train depot and
started off on their journey to the orphanage.
After two years there the boys came home again. Billy got a job as a
janitor. Besides sweeping floors and tending the fires, he had to get up
at two o'clock every morning and carry coal for fourteen stoves. For
this he received twenty-five dollars a month.

* Adapted from *Courage*, Regular Baptist Press. Used by permission.

What Billy loved more than anything else was baseball. He may have been the poorest boy in town, but he was the best ballplayer. Nobody could steal bases like Billy.

One day when Billy was twenty years old, Captain A.C. "Pop" Anson saw Billy playing in a game in his hometown. The famous leader of the Chicago White Stockings signed him to his team immediately.

Billy Sunday became a famous baseball player. The fans loved him because he made the game exciting. He could circle the bases in fourteen seconds. He was so fast his opponents usually threw wild in an effort to get the ball to the base before him.

Sunday became known as the fastest runner and the most daring base stealer in baseball. He played four years with the Chicago White Stockings. Then something happened that changed his life.

Although Billy had been taught to pray at his mother's knee and had gone to Sunday school as a boy, he had drifted far away from God. One Sunday afternoon he and some of his baseball buddies went into a saloon and drank enough liquor to make them act silly. They sat down on the curb across the street from the Pacific Garden Mission where some men and women were conducting a street meeting. When Billy heard the songs his mother used to sing he began to cry. One of the young men stepped out of the group and invited Billy Sunday to come down to the mission and get right with God.

Billy stood up and said to his pals, "We've come to the parting of our ways. I'm going to Jesus Christ."

Sunday left the group of baseball players and went to the Mission. That Sunday afternoon he became a Christian. He says of his conversion, "I staggered out of sin and into the arms of the Savior."

Billy didn't sleep a wink that night. He worried about going to practice at ten o'clock the next morning. Would his baseball friends make fun of him? Laugh or not, of one thing Billy was sure: he would be true to his newly found Savior.

Sunday was surprised when he arrived at the ball park the next morning. His friends didn't make fun of him. They wanted him to continue on the way he had started. They knew that he was right and they were wrong, but none of them had the courage to step out for Christ.

Billy began to tell others of Jesus as soon as he became a Christian. He also joined a church and faithfully attended Sunday services and prayer meetings. At one prayer meeting he met Helen Thompson, who later became his wife.

Sunday continued to play baseball with the White Stockings, but as a Christian he refused to play on Sundays. All his fans knew that he had become a Christian. After three years with Pittsburgh and Philadelphia baseball teams, Billy Sunday felt that God was leading him to retire from baseball and go into Christian work. Although the salary was less than twenty percent of what he earned as a baseball player, Billy took a job with the YMCA, helping to reach other young men for Christ.

After working hard with the YMCA, he took a job helping a famous evangelist, Wilbur Chapman. Billy wasn't much of a speaker in those days. He arranged the meetings, put up the big tent for the services, sold books, and took the collection.

One day Mr. Chapman decided to return to his church. Billy was out of a job. A small church in Iowa invited him to come to preach. After that, invitations kept coming. He held evangelistic meetings in many towns and large cities. God blessed him and helped him preach powerful sermons. People came out by the thousands to hear him, and hundreds put their trust in Jesus. In some places the saloons lost all their business when Billy Sunday came to town. When people found Jesus they didn't want to drink anymore.

Billy Sunday said it was important to decide to follow Christ early in life. The majority of people are converted before they are twenty. A few are saved between twenty and thirty, but after that the chances of becoming a Christian are slim. Hearts become too hard and don't want Jesus. Nevertheless, many boys and girls as well as their parents began to walk the road to heaven at his meetings.

The evangelist sometimes prayed in baseball terms. "Lord, bring people home to You. Some of them are dying on second and third base. Lord, have the people play the game of life right up to the limit so that home runs may be scored."

Billy Sunday not only learned how to play the game of baseball like a champion, but more important, he learned to play the game of life like a champion.

Questions for Thought:

1. What kind of a boyhood did Billy Sunday have?
2. What helped Billy decide to turn to Jesus?
3. How did his teammates treat him after he became a Christian?

4. Why did Billy give up his baseball career to take a much lower salary at the YMCA?
5. What sometimes happened in the cities where Billy Sunday preached?

Memory Verse: "I count all things to be loss in view of the surpassing value of knowing Christ Jesus my Lord" (Philippians 3:8).

Tiny Tot Verse: "That I may know Him" (Philippians 3:10).

NATURE CORNER: STRONG, COURAGEOUS, AND FREE

Long before the eagle became the national emblem of the United States, it was the symbol of the Persian and Roman armies. This powerful, majestic bird symbolizes strength, courage, and freedom. In 1782 the Continental Congress chose the bald eagle for our national emblem. The eagle appears on our dollar bills, coins, uniform buttons, medals, flag staffs, public documents, and the President's seal.

In the early days of our country, our national bird could be found in great numbers, but today it is nearly extinct. Because bald eagles were believed to be destructive birds of prey, many were killed. Even though a law was passed in 1940 to forbid the killing of bald eagles, they have become scarce for other reasons. Many of the trees where they make their homes have been cut down to make room for residential areas. The polluting of the lakes and rivers that they depended on for their food supply has also contributed to their decline.

Eagles build their nests, or eyries, in the top of tall trees near lakes, rivers, and streams. They gather branches and driftwood, some as long as five feet, and make huge nests lined with dried grasses, leaves, and moss. Eyries are at least four feet across and almost as deep, but one has been found that is ten feet by twelve feet.

Eagles mate for life. Papa even takes his turn at incubating the eggs. He is a good provider too and works hard to bring his eaglets fish and small animals to eat. He fiercely protects his family from other birds of prey.

The bald eagle is a huge, majestic bird with a wing span of seven feet. He soars high above the treetops, sometimes rushing downward in a steep nosedive to pounce on an animal for dinner.

Eagles are reluctant to leave their homes, but they are forced to when the streams and lakes freeze over and small animals disappear into their burrows. They fly just far enough south to find food. When spring comes, they eagerly make their way back to their homes, repair eyries that have been damaged by storms, and enlarge them. Sometimes they decorate their nests with man-made objects they may find, such as light bulbs or fish plugs. One eyrie that was found even had a tablecloth!

The year-old eaglets may come back to the eyrie the next spring too, but they are soon sent off to fend for themselves. It is time for a new family in that eyrie.

We admire the strong, courageous, freedom-loving bald eagle that symbolizes the goals and aspirations of our United States of America. The eagle also symbolizes the freedom and strength of the Christian. We read in Isaiah 40:31: "Yet those who wait for the Lord will gain new strength; they will mount up with wings like eagles, they will run and not get tired, they will walk and not become weary." If we spend time with God, reading His Word and praying, He can make us strong, courageous, and free.

Questions for Thought:

1. What bird is the national emblem of the United States?
2. On what objects do we find this emblem?
3. Why is the bald eagle nearly extinct today?
4. What is an eagle's nest like?
5. What is the most important characteristic of the eagle?
6. How can we as Christians be like eagles?

Memory Verse: "Yet those who wait for the Lord will gain new strength; They will mount up with wings like eagles, They will run and not get tired, They will walk and not become weary" (Isaiah 40:31).

Tiny Tot Verse: "Wait for the Lord" (Isaiah 40:31).

HYMN STORY: "BATTLE HYMN OF THE REPUBLIC"

"The Battle Hymn of the Republic" was written by Julia Ward Howe, a crusader for women's rights and a friend of President Abraham Lincoln. Visiting the site of a recent battle, Mrs. Howe heard Union soldiers singing around the campfire. She was especially touched by a song they sang about John Brown, who lost his life in his private war against slavery.

Mrs. Howe took the tune of the John Brown song and wrote new words for it, words that expressed faith and courage for the trying Civil War days. It became the marching song for the Union army and is still one of our nation's favorite patriotic songs. It is a song that honors God as well as country.

This song was sung by crowds of people when the train carrying President Eisenhower's body crossed the country. It was also sung when Robert Kennedy's body was brought by train from California. Julia Ward Howe's "Battle Hymn of the Republic" expresses the soul of the American people in times of tragedy as well as triumph.

Battle Hymn of the Republic

Mine eyes have seen the glory of the coming of the Lord;
He is trampling out the vintage where the grapes of wrath are stored;
He hath loosed the fateful lightning of His terrible swift sword;
His truth is marching on.

Chorus
Glory! glory, hallelujah! Glory! glory, hallelujah!
Glory! glory, hallelujah! His truth is marching on.

I have seen Him in the watchfires of a hundred circling camps;
They have builded Him an altar in the evening dews and damps;
I can read His righteous sentence by the dim and flaring lamps;
His day is marching on.

He has sounded forth the trumpet that shall never sound retreat;
He is sifting out the hearts of men before His judgment seat.
O be swift, my soul, to answer Him! be jubilant, my feet!
Our God is marching on.

In the beauty of the lilies, Christ was born across the sea,
With a glory in His bosom that transfigures you and me;
As He died to make men holy, let us die to make men free;
While God is marching on.

Discuss: "As He died to make men holy, let us die to make men free."

Memory Verse: "And you shall know the truth, and the truth shall make you free" (John 8:32).

Tiny Tot Verse: "The truth shall make you free" (John 8:32).

ACTIVITIES

Car Games

Alphabet Game. Each player tries to find the letters of the alphabet consecutively on signs along the roadside. The first one to reach *z* wins.

What Kind of Car? Each family member chooses a different make of car. He counts one point for each car of that kind he sees on the highway. The one with the most points wins. Variation: Each one chooses a state, excluding the one you're in. A point is earned for every car seen with a license plate from that state.

Bible Twenty Questions. Divide into two teams—the backseat versus the frontseat. Each team picks a person or object from the Bible. For instance, the backseaters choose Noah's ark. The frontseaters try to discover the answer by asking twenty questions. They begin by finding out if it is animal, vegetable, or mineral. They only ask questions which can be answered by a yes or a no.

Sign Game. Before your trip have your children make signs, or make them in the car. Let them choose from "Smile," "Wave," "Honk." Take turns showing the signs to passing motorists. If the person in the car responds to the sign and does what it says, the one who shows the sign gets a point.

Geography Game. The first player says the name of a city, river, country, or other geographical location. The next person has to say the name of a place beginning with the last letter of the previous place. For instance, if the first person says "Spain," the second might say "Nebraska," and the third "Annapolis."

Books of the Bible Review. Mom or Dad call out a book of the Bible and let the children tell you before you count to ten if it's in the Old or New Testament. When they become more skillful, ask them to name one of the major prophets before you count to ten, or a book of Moses. Then turn it around. Say, "First Chronicles"—the answer is History. Or "Job"—the answer is Poetry. Reviewing memory verses would be a wise use of time also. (*See* Bible Town in the May chapter for names of categories.)

Scavenger Hunt by Sight. Before starting out on your trip make a list of things to watch for and give points for each one.

1. A white horse-5

2. A windmill-3
3. A collapsed shed or barn-10
4. A California license plate-4
5. A colt-3
6. A lavender house-10
7. A lamb-6
8. A police car-3
9. A bumper sticker with a Christian message-10
10. A tractor-5
11. A travel trailer-2
12. A church-4

Make your own list with other ideas, or have your children write the list after you have started and decide on the number of points. Plan to play for a certain length of time, then add up the points to see who wins.

Patriotic Games

Game of the States. See how many states each family member can write on a slip of paper. Then test for the capitals of those states. Children may do better than their parents.

Game of the Flag. Answer the following questions about our flag:

1. When is Flag Day? (June 14)
2. What is our flag's nickname? (Old Glory)
3. What are the flag's three colors? (red, white, blue)
4. What do the colors represent? (blue, justice; white, purity; red, lifeblood of those willing to die for their country)
5. What does the flag at half-staff mean? (a high government official has died, or we are remembering men who died in battle)
6. What should be done with worn-out flags? (burned—destroyed with respect)
7. What famous song is about our flag? ("The Star-Spangled Banner")
8. How many white stripes on our flag? (six)
9. How many stars? (50)
10. What do the stars represent? (the number of states)

Fun with Puppets

Make puppets out of old socks, sewing on bright buttons for the eyes and nose. Sew on a mouth with red yarn, and use other colored yarn for hair.

Make puppets out of two paper plates put together with room in between for your hand. Paint or color a face on one of the paper plates. Use yarn for hair.

Use puppets to act out familiar stories or make up original skits. Encourage children to think of one they could give at Sunday school or children's church.

Treasure Hunt

This is especially fun for a lazy summer family evening or when you are out camping. Divide into two teams. Let Team One hide the treasure and Team Two find it. Devise clues that lead to the treasure's location. Encourage your children to think of clever clues—even rhyming ones, if possible. Have Dad on one side and Mom on the other to give guidance and ideas.

One clue leads to another until they finally reach the treasure, which can be any treat from balloons to popcorn balls. Then Team Two hides a treasure for Team One and thinks of clues.

Clues should be written on strips of paper and rolled up so they will not be easily detected. Tape a clue on a tree trunk, the outdoor water faucet, under the deck, under the swing, on the fence, under a flower pot—there are many interesting hiding places.

A clue leading to the outdoor water faucet might go like this:

> To find this clue, stop and think,
> It is where you take a drink.

A clue leading to under the flowerpot might be:

> My blossoms you can see,
> But look under me.

SOURCES

American Book of Days (New York: Bobley Publishing Corp., 1979).
William T. Ellis, *Billy Sunday* (Chicago: Moody Press, 1957).

Sigmund A. Lavine, *Wonders of the Eagle World* (New York: Dodd Mead and Co., 1974).

Amos R. Wells, *A Treasure of Hymns* (Boston: United Society of Christian Endeavor, 1914).

8

August

The early Romans must have run out of gods, goddesses, and festivals as names for the months of the year, because they resorted to numbering several of the months. Before the calendar was changed, August was simply "Sixth Month." When Caesar Augustus came into power he wanted a month named after him as July had been named in honor of his great-uncle and predecessor, Julius Caesar. Thus the eighth month of the year became August. Not content with that, the egotistical emperor decided his month should have as many days as his great-uncle's, so he stole a day from February to give August thirty-one days.

When we reach the eighth month we realize our year is more than half over. That makes us stop to think. What goals have we accomplished so far? School vacation is two-thirds over. Most parents probably heave a sigh of relief as they anticipate children going back to school. Just one month left!

There is another way to look at it. You have one month left before your child is put under the influence of another each weekday for the greater part of his waking hours. Now is your chance to teach and mold him. What can you teach him in the month of August?

August can be a boring month for children unless they go on vacation. Usually in August the scheduled activities of the summer taper off. This is your opportunity to advance some activities of your own that will be helpful to your child, teach him true values, and stimulate creativity. During this month encourage reading, go on family picnics, have long talks.

Think of August as your opportunity as a parent.

ESPECIALLY FOR PARENTS

"My mother never made me do any work at home, and that's why I have such a hard time keeping house now," complained a woman whose house usually looks a mess. Another woman attributed her dislike of housekeeping to the fact that as a member of a large family she had to work too hard when she was growing up.

Both extremes are harmful. Try to find the happy medium for your children: enough work to teach them responsibility and the satisfaction of completing a job, but not so much that they have no time for play and the other activities children need.

Work with Your Child

Working alongside your child makes an otherwise tedious chore a time of togetherness. Years ago whole neighborhoods worked together at threshing parties, roof-raisings, cornhuskings, and quilting bees. When the whole family is working together it can be fun.

I remember evenings during my childhood spent shelling the walnuts we raised to trade for groceries at a friend's store. During hot summer days I spent hours shelling peas, snipping beans, and husking corn for canning with my brother and sisters. Peeling apples and pears, washing jars—it was all part of our combined effort to put away food for the winter. What a difference when many hands do these time-consuming chores. I can still remember the feeling of satisfaction and accomplishment when I saw the jars all lined up on the table waiting to be taken to the cellar for future feasting.

Make Work Rewarding and Fun

It isn't nearly so hard to weed a long row of carrots if you are promised ice-cold lemonade and cookies when you are done. Small rewards for jobs well done produce incentive. How about giving a prize to the one who husks the most corn or snips the most beans?

Don't assign too big a job—it will only cause discouragement. Let a child do something fun after he has worked between half an hour and an hour. Children should probably not be paid for shouldering their share of household chores—that is part of their responsibility as members of the family. However, you might reward them with pay for other tasks outside the daily routine such as extra baby-sitting, yard work, or special projects.

What's wrong with making work fun? While cracking nuts, shelling peas, or peeling apples you can tell jokes and play games. Select an object in the kitchen and ask someone else to guess what it is simply by stating its color.

You can also make up a story in which one person says two or three sentences, then the next must add to it. It will probably turn out ridiculous, but it's lots of fun.

Many families make charts of chores, leaving spaces for gummed stars or a check when the job has been completed. This is usually for daily jobs such as making beds, hanging up clothes, and taking out garbage. A variation of that is to have a chart for Mom and Dad, too. Children do the checking or lick the stars for the parents.

By all means teach your children the value of work, the joys of accomplishing something, the satisfaction of a task well done. This will remain with them throughout their lives and be of untold benefit. An extra bonus is the help you as parents will receive when family members share the work load. Some parents protest that it's easier to do the work themselves than to train their kids to do it. That's true—it is a hassle at first until they learn—but later you will be well repaid for your trouble. Not only will they know how to take responsibility and be prepared for the future, but your home will run more smoothly as the work is divided among family members and not left entirely up to Mom and Dad.

For extra chores have a "work jar," which contains slips of paper with chores written on them. Family members draw a slip or two to find out what their extra chore or chores will be on a given day. This should eliminate the protest, "Susie never has to do anything."

FAMILY DEVOTIONS

BIBLE STUDY: LET'S PRAY ABOUT IT

Children usually have more faith than adults. They believe God's promises without reservations or doubts. I'm sure you have experienced marvelous answers to prayer in your family, perhaps as a reward of your children's faith rather than your own.

But what about the times when it seems God doesn't answer?

Sometimes God Says No

Amy Carmichael was a little English girl who lived many years ago. She looked at her brown eyes in the mirror. Why couldn't she have beautiful blue eyes like her mother? Suddenly she had an idea. Why not pray and ask God to change her brown eyes to blue? Mother said that God always hears and answers prayer.

Kneeling beside her bed, Amy asked God to change the color of her eyes. She then jumped into bed, confident that in the morning her eyes would be blue. As soon as she woke she ran to look in the mirror. To her great disappointment, her eyes were still brown. God hadn't answered. Then she heard a little voice in her heart say, "Isn't no an answer?"

Years later Amy Carmichael went to India as a missionary. She heard about children who were being sold to the priests and forced to live evil lives in the temples. God led her to establish a home for these mistreated children. To rescue them she disguised herself as an Indian by making her skin dark with coffee and by wearing a sari. She easily passed as an Indian woman and was allowed into the temples where foreigners were usually not permitted. If she'd had blue eyes, that would have been impossible.

God, who has a plan for each one of us, knew that Amy needed brown eyes, not blue. He said no to her prayer so that He could use her to rescue many temple children from a life of sin. Then she understood and was glad God had said no.

Questions for Thought

1. Why does God sometimes say no to our prayers?
2. Can you remember how one of God's no's turned out for the best?

Sometimes God Says Wait

Tell your children the story of the death of Lazarus as recorded in John 11:1-45. If your children are good readers, you may want to read it together. Ask the following questions:

1. Why didn't Jesus go to Lazarus immediately? (11:6)
2. What did Mary and Martha want Jesus to do? (11:21)
3. What better plan did Jesus have? (11:23)
4. What was the purpose of this trial? (11:4)
5. Can you see how Jesus turned a tragedy into a triumph?

6. Think of times when the answers to your prayers have been delayed. How was the delay for your good?

Often We Don't Understand

Don't make the mistake of trying to explain the unexplainable to your children. Admit that there are things you don't know. Point your children to the love, wisdom, power, and sovereignty of God. Teach them to trust Him even when they don't understand what He is doing. Read verses concerning prayer (Psalm 138:17-18; 147:5; Isaiah 55:8-9; Jeremiah 29:11; 31:3; Romans 8:28; 11:3; 1 Peter 5:7) and thanksgiving (Psalm 34:1; Ephesians 5:20; Colossians 4:2; 1 Thessalonians 5:18).

Encourage your child to keep a record of answers to prayers and not to forget to thank God for those answers. Inspire him to thank God for the things that cannot be understood, knowing that God is in control and will do what is best for His children.

Memory Verse: "For as the heavens are higher than the earth, so are My ways higher than your ways, and My thoughts than your thoughts" (Isaiah 55:9).

Tiny Tot Verse: "Ask and it shall be given to you" (Matthew 7:7).

A HEROINE TO FOLLOW: THE PRINCESS WHO BECAME A MISSIONARY

Maki wasn't interested in buying a new kimono. She already had more than she needed.

"Let's go home, Tomiko," she said to her maid, turning away from the bolts of bright-colored cloth. "I don't need another kimono."

"But your father said—" began the maid with a respectful bow.

"Never mind. Let's go home."

Maki felt cross. She was tired of shopping. She was tired of the useless activities her father insisted she do: arrange flowers, perform tea ceremonies, wear pretty clothes. Most of all she was tired of her father's nagging her to get married.

If only her mother were still living! Tears came to Maki's eyes as she thought of her mother's unhappiness concerning Father's taking other wives. But her mother had finally found comfort in becoming a Christian.

Maki was too independent to become a Christian, or yield to her father's wishes for her to marry a selfish, rich man like himself. She would rather not marry at all.

Mr. Hitotsuyanagi, Maki's father, was a feudal lord in Japan with great wealth and a high position. His daughter continually rebelled at his marriage plans for her. Finally he permitted her to study English at the Kobe University and later sent her to the United States for more schooling.

Maki learned many interesting things in America, such as the fact that hot dogs weren't made from dog meat, as she first imagined. She also made many friends. Most important of all, Maki found the Lord Jesus as her personal Savior and friend.

While Maki was studying in the United States, a very unusual young American man was teaching English in Japan. Merrell Vories went to Japan as a self-supporting missionary. After losing his teaching job for telling his students of Jesus Christ, he started both an architectural and a manufacturing business. He manufactured and sold mentholatum, which became known as "the Jesus salve" because Merrell included a leaflet about Jesus in every shipment. Merrell Vories soon gained a reputation for being an honest businessman who was unusually kind to his employees.

One day Maki's brother asked Vories to draw up plans for a building. By that time Maki had returned to Japan. Her brother asked her to help plan the building since she had been in the United States and knew about western-style architecture.

When Maki met Merrell she was immediately drawn to him. She liked his honesty. He seemed to be a man she could trust and love. Merrell was equally impressed with Maki and after several meetings wrote her asking her to marry him.

Maki wrote back that she would like to marry the young American, but her family would never permit her to do so. She was of the imperial household and could not marry a commoner, least of all a foreigner.

Merrell would not give up. Even though Maki's family fussed and fumed, they finally gave the necessary permission. Maki, the princess, became Mrs. Merrell Vories, the wife of an American missionary.

Maki's life as a missionary was quite different from that of a member of the imperial household. When she traveled with her husband on preaching tours, she often had to stay in run-down, rat-infested buildings. Even in her own home she had few of the luxuries and privacy she was used to.

But Maki had something else that made up for those hardships, something to live and work for. She brought girls into her home, taught them to clean and cook, and treated them like her daughters. She and her "daughters" cleaned up a vacant lot and made it into a playground for neglected children. They transformed a run-down house into a kindergarten. She started a primary school for working girls and became a friend to those in trouble. She also helped her husband in his efforts to tell people of Christ.

Cinderella was a poor girl who became a princess. Maki was a princess who chose to be a poor girl. But she wasn't really poor—she found a different kind of wealth in living a meaningful life for God and helping others.

Questions for Thought

1. Why was Maki bored with her life as a princess?
2. Why didn't she want to marry?
3. What attracted her to Merrell Vories?
4. Why was her life as a missionary better than as a princess?
5. If you are bored, what can you do? (Discuss ways your children can help others less fortunate than themselves.)

Memory Verse: "For whoever wishes to save his life shall lose it; and whoever loses his life for My sake and the gospel's shall save it" (Mark 8:35). (Explain how Maki gave up her luxuries to help others, and in doing so found joy and happiness. When we give up our own desires to do God's will and help others, we find joy and fulfillment.)

Tiny Tot Verse: "Love one another" (1 John 4:7).

NATURE CORNER: BALL OF FIRE

Did you know that the Campa Indians of Peru accept the sun as their best friend?* These Indians fear darkness more than wild beasts and enemies. They believe that the spirits of the dead roam the jungles at night, forever shut away from the light of the sun and the friendliness of a campfire.

Ancient peoples also worshiped the sun as the giver and sustainer of

---

* Adapted from *Challenge*, Regular Baptist Press. Used by permission.

life. We do not worship the sun but the One who created the sun. It is indeed a marvel of creation. Did you know that all of our weather (wind, snow, tornadoes, rain) is caused by the sun?

Did you know that the sun is the center of our solar system? Did you know that it provides our daily physical necessities? The sun raises the water from the rivers, lakes, and oceans through evaporation, then scatters the water over the thirsty land with rain, causing vegetation to grow. The sun activates the germ of life that lies in a seed to make it sprout. The sun provides energy for the green plants and trees to grow.

Did you know that the diameter of the sun is about one hundred times that of the earth, and that the sun could contain 330,000 earths?

Were you aware that the sun is ninety-three million miles from the earth? Calculating light traveling at 186,000 miles per second, the sun is eight and one third light minutes away from us. If the sun were farther away from the earth, everything here would freeze, and if it were closer, everything would burn. For hundreds of years the sun and the earth, as well as the other planets, have stayed in their courses, just the right distances apart, with no collisions or catastrophes.

Scientists have estimated the temperature on the sun's surface to be ten thousand degress. And we think it's hot at one hundred degrees! But that's not all—the temperature at the sun's center is thought to be about forty million degrees. Did you know that the heat of the sun is so great that if the earth fell into it, within a few minutes the earth would be completely vaporized?

The sun's rays come in different wave lengths which give rise to the colors of the rainbow (red, orange, yellow, green, blue, indigo, and violet). Combinations of those rays produce many more colors. Scientists tell us that each ray has a specific purpose for living things on earth.

We marvel at the engineering genius of our Creator. With the psalmist we exclaim, "The heavens declare the glory of God, and the firmament showeth his handiwork . . . in them hath he set a tabernacle for the sun . . . his going forth is from the end of the heaven, and his circuit unto the ends of it; and there is nothing hidden from the heat thereof" (Psalm 19:1, 4, and 6).

We worship Him who not only created the universe in all of its complexities, but also holds it up and keeps it running in perfect order. And to think that He's the one who comes to live in us when we receive Him as our Savior.

Questions for Thought:

1. How big is the sun compared to the earth?
2. What colors come from the sun?
3. What would happen to the earth if the sun were closer to us? Farther away?
4. Who keeps the sun just the right distance from the earth?

Memory Verse: "Thine is the day, Thine is the night; Thou hast established all the boundaries of the earth. Thou hast made summer and winter" (Psalm 74:16-17).

Tiny Tot Verse: "Thou hast made summer and winter" (Psalm 74:17).

HYMN STORY: "THE LOVE OF GOD"

Many years ago, we are told, the lyrics for the third verse of "The Love of God" were found written on the walls of an institution. Even before that, similar words were used in the Jewish Festival of Weeks and finally translated into English.

Frederick Lehman is the man who wrote the tune to this song and the lyrics to two of the verses. Mr. Lehman was the pastor of a small church, but had to also work in a cheese factory to support his family.

Mr. Lehman's wife often put verses in his lunch box along with his sandwiches. The day she put in the verse beginning, "Could we with ink the ocean fill . . ." her husband was so moved he came home from work and wrote a tune for it. Later he wrote the two additional verses.

The Love of God

The love of God is greater far than tongue or pen can ever tell;
It goes beyond the highest star, and reaches to the lowest hell.
The guilty pair, bowed down with care, God gave His Son to win;
His erring child He reconciled, and pardoned from his sin.

Chorus
Oh, love of God, how rich and pure! How measureless and strong!
It shall forevermore endure, the saints' and angels' song.

When hoary time shall pass away, and earthly thrones and kingdoms fall;
When men who here refuse to pray, on rocks and hills and mountains call;
God's love, so sure, shall still endure, all measureless and strong;
Redeeming grace to Adam's race—the saints' and angels' song.

Could we with ink the ocean fill, and were the skies of parchment made;
Were every stalk on earth a quill, and every man a scribe by trade;
To write the love of God above would drain the ocean dry,
Nor could the scroll contain the whole, tho' stretched from sky to sky.

Questions for Thought:

1. How does the songwriter describe God's love?
2. How long will God's love last?
3. How much ink would it take to write all there is to write about God's love?
4. Have you received God's love?

Memory Verse: "In this is love, not that we loved God, but that He loved us and sent His Son to be the propitiation for our sins" (1 John 4:10).

Tiny Tot Verse: "He loved us and sent His Son" (1 John 4:10).

ACTIVITIES

Outdoor Sing

You may want to invite other families to join yours for these activities, although they can be enjoyable for your family alone as well.

Lake Sing. Get into boats on a summer evening, push off into the water some distance, and sing favorite hymns and choruses. If someone plays the guitar or accordian, put them to work. Even without an instrument, singing praises to God on a lake as you watch the sunset will be an unforgettable experience for your family. If necessary, bring a hymnbook, but it's more fun to sing songs from memory.

Campfire Sing. Singing around a campfire is also a unique worship experience. Let children choose songs they know and enjoy. Learn a new chorus that is easy and fun to sing but that also has a message. Perhaps your Sing will develop into a time of sharing private thoughts and experiences with the Lord. Roast marshmallows for a treat, or have s'mores (a toasted marshmallow and a section of Hershey's candy bar between graham cracker halves).

Family Hikes

Hikes are especially fun if Mom and Dad go too. Make your hike more meaningful when you return by asking each family member to talk about three things that he noticed as he walked along. This will help your children become more observant as well as help them learn to express themselves.

Unfortunately, some of us live too far away from wooded areas to enjoy real nature hikes. If this is true of your family, go to a city park instead. If this is not feasible, take walks together through an unexplored neighborhood.

Take turns deciding which direction you will turn when you get to a corner. Talk about the trees and flowers you pass, or discuss the architecture of the buildings. Watch for birds and try to identify them.

Just the fact that you go with your kids will make the walk meaningful to them.

Scavenger Hunt

Give your children a list of items they are to find in the area where you are camping or picnicking. The items will vary according to where you are, but here is a suggested list:

maple leaf	toad	acorn
pine cone	cocoon	fern
rock	shell	moss
bird feather	dandelion	stick

Dividing into teams makes it more fun. The team that comes up with all the items first wins.

Backyard Bible Baseball

This game can be played at any outdoor area with enough space. Set up the bases and divide into two teams. Ask quiz questions of the first team. If they get the answer right they take a base. If they miss, it's one out for their team. Only the players that make it home score points. After three outs the other side gets its turn at the plate. Keep score as you would in a regular baseball game.

Some suggested questions:

1. Who was the first man? (Adam)
2. To whom did the angels announce the birth of Jesus? (shepherds)
3. Which disciple denied Jesus? (Peter)
4. Name the man Jesus brought back to life after he had been dead four days. (Lazarus)
5. Who was the very first baby? (Cain)
6. Who was the father of the Jewish nation? (Abraham)
7. Who was Adam's wife? (Eve)
8. How many sons did Jacob have? (12)
9. How many apostles did Jesus have? (12)
10. What king wanted to kill the baby Jesus? (Herod)
11. What baby was hidden in the bulrushes of the river? (Moses)
12. Who had a coat of many colors? (Joseph)
13. Who betrayed Jesus? (Judas)
14. Who was the mother of Jesus? (Mary)
15. Who killed the giant Goliath? (David)
16. Who was thrown in the lion's den? (Daniel)
17. Who was Israel's first king? (Saul)
18. Who was the tax collector who became a disciple of Jesus? (Matthew)
19. How many loaves and fishes did the little boy give to Jesus? (5 loaves, 2 fishes)
20. How many people did Jesus feed with the boy's lunch? (5000)
21. Who led Israel out of Egypt? (Moses)
22. Who led Israel into the Promised Land? (Joshua)
23. Who was Abraham's wife? (Sarah)
24. What animal did Jesus ride when He came into Jerusalem? (donkey)
25. What animal did Satan enter in the Garden of Eden? (serpent)
26. What other animal is Satan likened to in the Bible? (lion)
27. What Jewish girl became queen of Persia? (Esther)
28. Who was Naomi's daughter-in-law? (Ruth)
29. Who turned into a pillar of salt? (Lot's wife)
30. Who was almost offered as a human sacrifice? (Isaac)
31. Who was Mary's husband? (Joseph)
32. Name the city whose walls fell down when Israel marched around it. (Jericho)

33. How many people were crucified with Jesus? (two)
34. Who was struck blind on his way to Damascus? (Saul, Paul)

Easy Nature Questions:

1. Name a bird with a red breast. (robin)
2. Name a land creature that is guided to his food by echoes. (bat)
3. Name an insect noted for its busyness. (bee)
4. Name a sly animal. (fox)
5. Name the creature who spins a web. (spider)
6. What tame animal can see in the dark? (cat)
7. What animal is called "King of the Beasts"? (lion)
8. Which has brighter feathers, a male or female bird? (male)
9. Why do female birds wear duller colors? (for protection when on their nests)
10. What bird is considered wise? (owl)
11. What fish swims upstream to spawn? (salmon, carp)
12. What creature eats dirt? (earthworm)
13. What does a butterfly start out as? (caterpillar)
14. What creature changes its colors? (chameleon)
15. What insect produces light? (firefly)
16. What is a baby frog called? (tadpole)
17. Name an animal that carries his home with him. (hermit crab, snail)
18. Name an animal that builds dams. (beaver)
19. Name an animal that stores nuts for the winter. (squirrel)
20. What animal is considered man's best friend? (dog)
21. What creature damages forests and feeds on buildings? (termites)
22. What sea animal navigates by emitting sounds? (dolphins)
23. What sea creature can grow lost limbs? (starfish)
24. What animal peculiar to northern regions drowns itself in the sea? (lemming)
25. What kind of dogs do Eskimos use to pull their sleds? (huskies)

Tenting in the Backyard

Everyone can't go camping, at least not as often as they would like. Putting a tent up in the backyard is almost as fun, especially if the children are allowed to sleep in it. If you don't have a tent, how about letting your children use an old blanket? Drape it over the clothesline or the picnic table.

Even if you dare not leave them there overnight and hesitate to give up your comfortable bed to join them, you can put up tents for daytime and evening fun. Play games and tell stories in the tent with your children. Stories of your childhood antics are fun.

Sea, Air, Land

Form a circle. The person chosen "It" throws a knotted handkerchief to someone and shouts out either "sea," "land," or "air." The one who catches the handkerchief must say the name of a specific creature that lives in the place called. Just saying "fish" or "bird" is not good enough. If the person does not answer correctly before "It" has counted to ten, he becomes "It" and throws the handkerchief to somebody else in the circle.

SOURCES

George Douglas, *American Book of Days* (New York: H.W. Wilson Co., 1937).

Grace Nies Fletcher, *The Bridge of Love* (New York: Dutton and Co., Inc., 1967).

Clifford B. Hicks, *The World Above* (New York: Holt, Rinehart and Winston, 1965).

Frank Houghton, *Amy Carmichael of Dohnavur* (London: S.P.C.K., 1954).

George Beverly Shea with Fred Bauer, *Songs That Lift the Heart* (Old Tappan: Fleming H. Revell, 1972).

9

September

September means "seventh" in Latin. September was once the seventh month on the calendar. Even though September is now the ninth month of the year, the name has remained.

Labor Day is celebrated on the first Monday of September, a time to commemorate the labor movement in our country. Most families use the holiday for one last vacation before the fall routine begins.

School starts in September. The fall schedule at church begins. Most of us feel a sense of purpose with vacations behind us and work before us. We encourage our children to face their new school and church year with anticipation and enthusiasm.

On September 25 Jewish people celebrate the Festival of Booths, which commemorates God's commanding His people to live in booths, or temporary shelters, to remind them of their journey through the wilderness as well as their temporary stay on this earth.

A full moon shines at the time of the autumnal equinox as summer gives place to fall. This is sometimes called the harvest moon. In Taiwan the people celebrate this full moon with a festival, preparing moon-shaped cakes and eating them outdoors in the moonlight.

Many of us take part in harvesting vegetables and fruits during these last days before the frost comes. What a blessing to be able to put away food for the winter months ahead.

The crisp mornings and evenings of September remind us that winter is coming. Like the virtuous woman of Proverbs 31, we are not afraid of the snow because we are ready.

ESPECIALLY FOR PARENTS

September again and time for school. That means new clothes, shoes, school supplies, and money for school lunches. For some it means tuition if your children attend a private school. How can you meet all these extra expenses?

No doubt you have planned for these extra items, but even so they may seem overwhelming at today's prices. But don't panic, sending Mom scurrying out to find a job, until you have explored the alternatives. Sit down and think of ways you can economize.

Food

The biggest item for any family after housing is food. We have to eat, although sometimes we wish we didn't when the checkout girl at the supermarket tallies up our bill. There are ways, however, to stretch our food dollars.

Make Things from Scratch. I know this isn't a popular idea. It's so convenient to grab a mix and have a dish ready to serve minutes later, but remember, you are paying for that convenience. You are paying for someone else's work. Although I don't think I'll ever wean myself away from the cake mixes that turn out light and delicious, I can make other things from scratch: pie crust, cookies, biscuits, muffins, pancakes, salad dressings, soups. It is really quite simple to do this, and the results are often more tasty than the mixes.

Stretch the Meat. Health experts tell us that Americans eat too much meat. Meat is an expensive item and should be stretched both for economical and health reasons. Soups, stews, and stir-fry dishes do not require a great amount of meat in order for them to be delicious. Use less meat and more vegetables for nutritious, thrifty eating. Also use healthful meat substitutes—eggs, cheese, beans.

Eliminate Junk Food. Carbonated beverages, potato chips, and candy taste wonderful; however, they are not only expensive but also detrimental to your health. Except for an occasional treat, why not eliminate these items and other junk food from your shopping list? You'll have more dollars for the nutritious food your family needs. Fruits are a good substitute for junk food.

Freeze and Can. If you had a garden this summer, or if you have friends with gardens, you will be able to put away vegetables for the winter. Each area of our country has special fruits that can be canned or dried for delightful winter eating. In Washington state, blackberries grow in abundance along roadsides and in wooded areas. They can be made into delicious sauces, pies, and jams. Other areas have different specialties that can be preserved for winter eating. Besides being taste treats, these items help your food budget.

Resist the Temptation to Eat Out. It's fun to go to a restaurant as a family once in a while, but you can make eating at home festive too. Eat at the dining room table for a change and decorate with lighted candles to make the occasion special. You can make a roast beef dinner for half of what it would cost in a restaurant, and have some meat left over for hash. By dressing up the table a bit and using your good dishes, you'll get the feeling of "eating out" but won't have to pay the exorbitant prices. Dad might even want to do the dishes to make it extra special.

The same goes for hamburgers at a fast-food place. It's very little work to broil or fry hamburger patties at home and put them on buns. You can even make your own french fries for a fraction of what they cost store-bought.

I rebelled when my husband insisted we make our own ice-cream cones instead of buying them at the ice-cream shop, until I realized how much money we would save. Ice-cream cones don't cost a nickel anymore.

Some families eat out so often it's no wonder they can't make ends meet. Eating out has become so widespread it has been jokingly suggested that if this trend continues Bobby will soon be saying, "Oh, goody, we get to eat at home for my birthday!"

Of course you'll want to eat out for an occasional treat, but resist the temptation to do it too often if you want to keep your budget balanced.

Cut Down on Waste

My daughter-in-law cut her paper napkins in half when she lived in Japan and was on a stringent budget. My husband and I use ours more than once. I read in a magazine that if you use a roll of paper towels a week you are extravagant. I concentrate on using mine wisely and find I can make a roll last a whole month.

Here are a few tips to help out the food budget.

1. Make whole milk and powdered milk into a 50/50 mixture.
2. Try using generic brands of food.

3. Avoid individually packed snacks for lunches. Buy in bulk and divide into smaller portions yourself.
4. Buy sale items in bulk if they are non-perishable.
5. Reuse aluminum foil.
6. Butter only one slice of bread when making a sandwich. Put filling on the other.
7. Make use of fruits and vegetables you grow yourself or get from friends.
8. Don't let food spoil.

Many people are turning out lights and turning down the heat, especially at night. Wood stoves are becoming increasingly popular as the price of oil and electricity go up. Americans are learning to economize.

Here are a few other hints that may help your budget:

1. Plan ahead so you can write letters instead of making long distance phone calls.
2. Watch the sales for food and clothing bargains.
3. Watch the want ads for good used furniture or other necessary items.
4. Check out garage sales for items you need (but don't fall into the trap of buying white elephants!).
5. Don't go window-shopping too often. You may be tempted to buy something you don't need.
6. Don't go grocery shopping when hungry.
7. Use coupons for discounts.
8. Trade baby-sitting with friends.
9. Carpool whenever possible.
10. Make gifts instead of buying them.

Teach Your Children to Economize and Share

When we scold our children for leaving food on their plate because half the people in the world are starving, we only make them feel guilty. They can't send what's left on their plate halfway around the world. Better to give them concrete ways they can help people in need.

How about letting your family suggest something you will go without for a week or a month in order to send money to victims of an earthquake or famine? Perhaps you can save dimes for a month or two to help build a hospital in India or use the proceeds from a family garage sale to help support a Korean orphan.

Economizing, not only to better their own situation but to share with others in need, is a beautiful scriptural concept to instill into your children.

FAMILY DEVOTIONS

BIBLE STUDY: GOD PROVIDES FOR ELIJAH AND FOR US
(1 KINGS 17)

Elijah the prophet was concerned about his people because they had forsaken God to worship idols. He asked God to withhold rain to make the people think and return to Him.

When he announced to wicked King Ahab that there would be no rain for a long, long time, the king was angry and wanted to capture him. But God told Elijah about a good hiding place by a little brook. God promised to send food to him by ravens.

Every morning and every evening the ravens came with bread and meat for Elijah. Where do you think they got this food?

One day, because there was no rain, the brook dried up. Elijah couldn't live without water. What could he do? God, who always takes care of His children, had a plan for Elijah. He told Elijah to stay with a widow in Zarephath of Sidon, a country bordering Israel.

When Elijah reached the widow's house she was gathering sticks to make a fire to cook the last food she had for her son and herself. Elijah asked her to make him a little bread first, and if she did, her food would not run out until the rains came back to make food grow again.

The widow did as Elijah asked her and made the bread. There was enough flour and oil left to make bread for her son and her, too. Every day when she came to the bowl of flour and jar of oil there was enough to make bread. God kept His promise and provided for Elijah and the widow's needs.

Read what Jesus says about this in Matthew 6:25-34 and Luke 12:6-7. Talk about God's provision for the plants and the birds and especially for His children. God has promised not only to supply our physical needs but all our needs. What needs do you have today?

Read the following promises:

1. Wisdom, James 1:5
2. Strength, 2 Corinthians 12:9
3. Grace, 2 Corinthians 9:8

Memory Verse: "And my God shall supply all your needs according to His riches in glory in Christ Jesus" (Philippians 4:19).

Tiny Tot Verse: "God shall supply all your needs" (Philippians 4:19).

HERO TO FOLLOW: WHAT HAPPENED TO GEORGE?

George was an expert thief.* Even though his father, a Prussian tax-collector, gave him plenty of spending money, he always wanted more. One day when he was ten years old, he stole some of his father's tax money and hid it in his shoe. His father searched his pockets and found nothing, but he was sure his son had stolen the money.

"Take off your shoes," he demanded.

George reluctantly removed his shoes. Sure enough, there was the money.

Caught! George apologized and promised not to steal again, but he did not keep his promise. One day when he was sixteen years old he ran up bills at two expensive hotels, then tried to escape through the window without paying. He was caught again. That time he landed in jail for twenty-four days.

George's father wanted him to become a minister. In Prussia in those days there were few ministers who really knew God. George certainly did not, but he thought being a minister would be a good job, so he began to study.

Even though George studied hard, he never read the Bible. In between his studies he and his friend Beta kept up their drinking, dishonesty, and wild adventures.

But something happened to Beta. He became a genuine Christian and started going to prayer meetings instead of parties. One evening he invited George to go with him, and George agreed. At the meeting he felt uneasy, yet interested. After singing a hymn, one of the young men knelt down and began to pray aloud. George was twenty-one years old, but had never before seen a man on his knees praying to God. The sight of it made him feel wistful, and suddenly he wanted to be like his friend Beta and the young man who was praying. He wanted what they had.

As they walked home after the meeting that evening, George said to

* Adapted from *Proteen,* Light and Life Press. Used by permission.

Beta, "All our former pleasures are as nothing compared to what we experienced tonight." He could hardly wait until it was time for the next meeting.

George found out as he kept going to the meetings that Jesus would come into his life just as He had come into Beta's. All he had to do was believe and ask the Savior. How happy he was after he invited Jesus into his life and received the forgiveness of his sins. Gradually he left his old ways and began to follow Jesus in earnest. He began to read the Bible and learned to pray.

He did not know at that time that God was preparing him for a very special task. God has a special plan for each one of His children. As part of that plan, God led George to stay at an orphanage in Prussia while he completed his pastoral studies at Halle University.

George was very impressed by this orphanage because its founder, Mr. Francke, supported it only by prayer. He trusted God to supply the money for the orphans.

George Mueller eventually became a pastor in England and helped many people find Jesus. But the homeless children on the streets bothered him. He remembered Mr. Francke's orphanage in Prussia and felt that God wanted him to start a similar one in England.

Mueller was a poor man, but he had a very wealthy God. He started his orphanage trusting in God to supply the necessary money. God honored George's prayers and faith. He always provided for the needs of the orphans. One morning there was no food for breakfast and no money to buy it. George was sure that God would not let the orphans go hungry. As he went out for an early morning walk, he met a man who gave him a gift of money for the orphans. George joyfully spent the money for food, and the orphans had their breakfast as usual. God always supplied in the nick of time. He was never too late.

George Mueller eventually had five orphan homes in Bristol, England, which sheltered over 2,000 children. Because he not only provided them with food, clothing, shelter, and education, but also taught them of his Savior, Jesus, many of the orphans became Christians.

Mueller lived to be ninety-three years old. People from all over the world knew about him and his orphan homes. More than that, they knew about his faithful God who always answered prayer. George Mueller demonstrated to the world that God is indeed real and would never disappoint those who put their trust in Him.

What happened to George the thief? God came into his life, and the same thing can happen to you. He may not lead you to start orphanages, but He has something wonderful planned for you.

Questions for Thought:

1. What kind of a boy was George?
2. What happened to him when he was twenty-one?
3. What did God call him to do?
4. How were the orphanages financed?
5. What plan do you think God has for you?

Memory Verse: "But seek first His kingdom and His righteousness; and all these things shall be added unto you" (Matthew 6:33).

Tiny Tot Verse: "Seek first His kingdom" (Matthew 6:33).

NATURE CORNER: GOD DESIGNED SLEEP

God designed sleep. It is a time to rest the body and mind. When we sleep our muscles relax, our heartbeat slows down, and our body temperature drops. Scientists tell us that the brain remains active during sleep, but that the activity is different from when we are awake.

Sleep is necessary for good health. People who don't sleep become irritable. If they go without sleep for a long period of time, they become unable to think clearly and may lose their memory or become mentally ill.

God made the night for people to sleep. During the day our earth faces the sun, but during the night it is shaded from the sun. This is God's heating and cooling system. It is also His plan for man's sleep. It is easier for most of us to sleep when it is dark outside. When we sleep the people on the other side of the world are awake and busy. When daytime comes to us, darkness comes to them, and it is their turn to sleep.

Animals sleep, too. Nobody knows for sure if simpler animals, such as crabs, sleep, but they do rest from their activities. Even the cells of plants take a rest. Many creatures rest or sleep during the daytime and use the night hours to forage for food. The psalmist wrote: "Thou dost appoint darkness and it becomes night, in which all the beasts of the forest prowl about. The young lions roar after their prey, and seek their food from God" (Psalm 104:20-21).

If you go outside at night, especially in the summertime, you will hear frogs chirping and owls hooting. You may see fireflies or bats darting about. In the fields and forests other animals are looking for food.

Some animals sleep most of the winter when the weather is cold and food is scarce. That is called hibernation.

Most people sleep about seven or eight hours a day. Alfred the Great, a ninth-century English king, decided that his subjects should divide their days into three eight-hour periods: eight hours for work, eight hours for play, and eight hours for sleep. This idea still persists today.

Did you know that cats sleep sixteen hours a day? They take "cat naps" all day long. Birds sleep at night. They stop singing if you drape something over their cage to make it dark. Wild birds usually begin to sing at dawn.

Most animals have a particular place to sleep even if it is only a hole in a log. The parrotfish of the West Indies makes an "instant bedroom" to sleep in, which is a cocoon spun from gooey material that he carries in his body.

Aren't you glad you have a cozy place to sleep every night? When you go to bed you say "good night," which is really a wish that your family will have a good night as they sleep under God's watchful care.

God provides all our needs. One of them is sleep. Can you name other needs we have that God supplies?

Questions for Thought:

1. When do most people sleep? Animals? Birds?
2. What happens to our mind and body when we sleep?
3. What happens to people who don't sleep enough?
4. Why did God design sleep?
5. What does "good night" really mean?

Memory Verse: "In peace I will both lie down and sleep, for Thou alone, O Lord, doest make me dwell in safety" (Psalm 4:8).

Tiny Tot Verse: "In peace I will ... sleep" (Psalm 4:8).

HYMN STORY: "I'D RATHER HAVE JESUS"

George Beverly Shea, well-known gospel singer, was brought up in a minister's home where singing was daily fare. His mother woke the family up every morning by singing and playing "Singing I Go." George later used this favorite gospel hymn as the theme song for his radio program, "Hymns from the Chapel."

Because of his parents' interest in music, George was privileged to meet a number of famous songwriters during his boyhood days. When he became a teenager his mother encouraged him to sing solos and to play the organ in church.

Even though George believed in Christ as a boy, he never confessed Him openly as his Savior until he was eighteen years old. He waited until the very last night of the special meetings at his church but at last overcame his shyness and walked forward to publicly surrender to Christ as the audience sang the hymn "Just As I Am."

George's mother collected poems, and one day she left one on the piano for George to see. It was Rhea F. Miller's "I'd Rather Have Jesus." George, impressed by the words, composed a tune for them and sang his new composition that day in church. Since that time George Beverly Shea has sung that particular song perhaps more than any other.

I'd Rather Have Jesus

I'd rather have Jesus than silver or gold
　　I'd rather be His than have riches untold,
I'd rather have Jesus than houses or lands,
　　I'd rather be led by His nail-pierced hands.

Chorus
Than to be the king of a vast domain,
　　Or be held in sin's dread sway.
I'd rather have Jesus than anything
　　This world affords today.

I'd rather have Jesus than men's applause,
　　I'd rather be faithful to His dear cause,
I'd rather have Jesus than worldwide fame,
　　I'd rather be true to His holy name.

This may be a good time to explain to your child that Jesus wants to be his personal Savior but that He will only come into his life by being invited. You may feel led to help your children pray a simple prayer like this: "Dear Lord, I want You too. Please forgive my sins and come into my life. Thank You for dying on the cross for me. I want to follow You more than anything."

Memory Verse: "For what does it profit a man to gain the whole world, and forfeit his soul?" (Mark 8:36).

Tiny Tot Verse: "Have faith in God" (Mark 11:22).

ACTIVITIES

Playing Store

Playing store can begin on a family night when parents can get into the fun with the children. No doubt the children will continue this activity on their own indoors on rainy afternoons or outdoors with neighborhood friends on a fine day.

Begin ahead of time to save empty boxes such as margarine cartons, cereal boxes, and cracker boxes. Save paper sacks, too, so the "storekeeper" can pack up his customers' purchases just as they do in real stores.

Make play money. Cut out paper bills. Use various sized buttons for coins, covering them with tape and marking the denomination with ink.

Make shelves by stacking boxes on top of one another. Wooden crates are best, but cardboard cartons will do.

Play food can be made out of clay or play dough. It's fun to shape small bananas, oranges, and so on. When playing store outdoors, rocks make fine potatoes, and sand works for flour, sugar, and salt. Small jars with screw tops that you usually throw away make excellent containers as do empty shortening cans. Children can return their purchases to the store after they finish playing. Keep the supplies in the boxes.

Guess the Cost

Cut advertisements for various products from magazines and newspapers. Write the price on the back. Let each family member guess the price. The one closest to the price gets the ad. The one with the most ads at the end of the game is the winner and should get to choose the treat. This game will teach your children something about the value of things.

Think Fast Game

The leader says the name of a city, points to someone, and counts to ten. The one pointed to must say the state, where the city is located before the leader reaches ten. If he does not, he becomes the leader. A variation requires the leader to say the name of a state, and the one pointed to must name a city in that state. There are several possible variations of that game.

Sardines

This is a reversed game of hide-and-seek. "It" hides by himself while the others count to thirty and then go looking for him. The first one to find him joins him in his hiding place. When another member finds them, he crowds in too. Soon the family members are packed together like sardines. The last one to find the rest of the family becomes "It" for the next game. This is hilarious, especially if the hiding place is in a small closet or under a bed.

Hide the Thimble

One player goes out of the room. The other players put a thimble or other small object somewhere in the room where it can be seen but not very easily. The player comes back in the room and begins to search. To guide him in his search the players shout "hot" when he gets near the object and "cold" when he walks farther away from it. At last he finds it, and someone else goes out to take a turn. Small children especially enjoy this.

Keepaway

The boys against the girls in this game if there are even numbers of each. If not, choose sides. Make sure Dad and Mom are on opposite teams. Play outdoors with a rubber ball that is easy to catch or in the recreation room with a pair of rolled-up socks. The team with the ball tries to keep the other team from intercepting it while they toss it back and forth.

Late Picnic

Have one last picnic before the weather gets too cold. Make a pizza and buy fruit for a fun supper in the park. Dress warmly. If the weather is too cool, eat in the car while enjoying the fall colors in the park. A rousing game of Follow the Leader or Keepaway would be fun and warm everyone up.

SOURCES

Margaret Cooper and Inda Mantel, *The Balance of Living* (New York: The Natural History Press, 1971).

Deluxe Appointment Book (New York: Bobley Publishing Corp., 1980).

Richard Deming, *Sleep* (New York: Thomas Nelson Inc., 1972).

James Gilchrist Lawson, *Deeper Experiences of Famous Christians* (Anderson: Warner Press, 1911).

A.T. Pierson, *George Mueller of Bristol* (Chicago: Moody Press).

10

October

Although October is the tenth month in our year, it is translated from the Latin word for "eighth month." The name was not changed when Julius Caesar made October the tenth month on the calendar.

October is mostly thought of as being the month of Halloween. Many parents endure rather than enjoy this holiday that necessitates scrounging up costumes for children and buying large supplies of treats for an endless line of trick or treaters on Halloween night.

Years ago, people were genuinely frightened by the spirits who were said to roam the countryside on All Hallow's Eve. A bellringer was hired in Brittany to go about warning people that ghosts were coming.

Real witches frightened people as well. These women, dressed in black, practiced magic and cast spells. The wealthy witches could afford to ride to their meetings on horseback, but the poorer ones had to walk. Because some carried long sticks or brooms to help them vault over streams, people imagined that they rode through the sky on broomsticks.

In days past, people wore hideous masks to prevent ghosts from recognizing them and doing them harm. Our Halloween masks today are to disguise us from neighbors and friends and are worn just for fun.

Besides being the month we celebrate Halloween, October is famous for several historical events: William the Conqueror taking over England; Columbus discovering America; the debut of the Model T Ford;

the launching of Sputnik; and the celebration of the Protestant Reformation.

ESPECIALLY FOR PARENTS

Talk to any number of adults and you will hear a variety of stories about childhood fears. Some of my friends confided that they were afraid to put their feet clear to the bottom of the bed because snakes crawled there at night, and if a leg accidentally draped over the edge of the bed it would surely be snapped off by a crocodile.

When I was a child my sister, just a bit older than I, informed me that every truck that went past our house was driven by a kidnapper. The famous Lindbergh baby had recently been kidnapped, and since we had a bachelor neighbor named Lindbergh, we children imagined that this horrible event had taken place right in our neighborhood instead of four thousand miles away. So the fear of kidnappers usually kept me indoors until my brother and sisters came home from school. Besides that I had to put up with fierce bears who lived under our house! My unsuspecting mother couldn't figure out why I didn't want to play outside—she thought I didn't like fresh air. Many children suffer from secret fears. Could that be why many children fight bedtime so vehemently?

At a Bible Camp in California several years ago a woman and her daughter were awakened one night when someone shouted, "Don't shoot him in the head!" Certain that the camp had been invaded by killers, they fled into the forest, dressed only in their nightclothes. For two weeks they eluded pursuers they were certain wanted to murder them. When they were finally rescued, they discovered that there was no murder plot—one of the camp's staff had been forced to kill a raccoon for fear he was rabid and someone had shouted, "Don't shoot him in the head." The woman and her daughter had risked dying of exposure and starvation because of ungrounded, unreasonable fears.

While many of our phobias are just as unreasonable, they are very real to us and can be paralyzing. Children are frightened by spooky television programs or by scenes of wars, crimes, fires, and calamities viewed on newscasts.

Children also catch the moods of adults who are worried about inflation, government corruption, inequities, lawlessness, terminal illnesses, and other problems. Our fears are contagious.

God gives the remedy for fear in His Word. Someone has said there are over 365 "Fear nots" in the Bible, one for every day of the year! We need to memorize those wonderful verses, meditate upon them, apply them to our lives, and share them with our children.

FAMILY DEVOTIONS

BIBLE STUDY: FEAR NOT

Have your family members write down some things they are afraid of. Then show them from God's Word why such fears are unnecessary. The Bible has much to say about our fears of: the dark (Genesis 1:4-5; Isaiah 41:13); thunder and storms (Psalm 107:25, 29); ridicule (Isaiah 2:22; 51:7-8); bad people (Job 1:12; 2:6; Matthew 10:28); nuclear war (Psalm 46:1-3); and death (2 Corinthians 5:1-9; Philippians 1:21-23; 1 Thessalonians 4:16-18).

Never make fun of a child's fears. To him they are real and terrifying. Let him talk them out and show him promises from God's Word. Other "fear not" verses:

Joshua 1:9	Matthew 14:27
Psalm 56:11; 91:5	Luke 2:10; 12:7, 32
Proverbs 3:24	Revelation 1:17
Isaiah 12:2; 43:1; 51:7	

Memory Verse: "Do not fear, for I have redeemed you; I have called you by name; you are Mine!" (Isaiah 43:1).

Tiny Tot Verse: "I have called you by name" (Isaiah 43:1).

A HERO TO FOLLOW: NOT GOOD ENOUGH

Martin Luther was not happy as a child. He had worries. He tried hard to be good, but sometimes he was bad. He worried constantly that God would punish him.

Martin studied law because his father wanted him to be a lawyer. But he felt very restless—he found the Bible more interesting than his law books.

When the Black Plague struck his town and many people died, Martin became frightened. Was God angry with him? When a bolt of lightning nearly struck him he was sure God was angry with him and promised that he would become a monk.

Martin Luther tried hard to be a good monk. Sometimes he whipped his body and lay for hours on a cold, bare stone floor. He often fasted and said many prayers. He hoped that by doing those things he would gain favor with God and get rid of his sins. But they did not bring him the peace he desperately wanted.

Luther was so interested in reading the Bible his fellow monks gave him his own copy. There was one verse in the Bible that he read over and over again: "The just shall live by faith" (Romans 1:17). Was it faith that God wanted instead of works?

Gradually, as he read the Bible, Martin Luther understood that the answer certainly was faith and not works. Neither giving money to the church, nor performing good deeds, not even climbing on your knees up Pilate's stairway in Rome was the remedy. The solution was in that Bible verse: "The just shall live by faith."

That means we are saved from sin not by *doing,* but by *believing* in what Jesus did for us on the cross. We can never do enough good things to pay for our sins. That's why Jesus had to die. He paid for our sins in our place. If we receive Him as our Savior, God receives us as His sons.

Martin Luther recorded his beliefs and posted them on the door of the church at Wittenberg as was the custom when someone wished to start a debate. Not only the church leaders, but people all over Germany were soon discussing what Martin Luther had written. Most of the church's leaders opposed him.

One day when Martin Luther was on a journey to Wittenberg, armed riders surrounded his cart. Many of his followers had feared for his life because he dared to oppose the pope and other officials. Was this to be his end?

His assailants put Luther on a horse and commanded that he come with them. To Luther's surprise his captors led him to Wartburg Castle. They were not enemies trying to harm him but friends trying to protect him. Prince Frederick the Wise had ordered the kidnapping for Luther's own safety. He was to disguise himself as a knight and continue his writing at the castle.

For many months Luther worked on writing pamphlets and translating the New Testament into German. After about a year of hiding he could stand it no longer. He had to return to the people and continue to fight for the truth. Frederick allowed him to leave the castle and go to Wittenberg to continue his reform work.

Although his writings were burned and he was in danger for many years, he sustained his brave stand for the truth. Through him and other fearless reformers, the Protestant Reformation took place. We celebrate this event each year on the last Sunday of October.

The reformers taught that:

1. Salvation is by faith, not by works.
2. Every believer can go directly to God through Jesus.
3. The Bible is for everyone to read and understand.

When Martin Luther understood these truths, he no longer felt uncertain and unhappy. He was sure that Jesus had taken care of his sins. He spent the rest of his life pastoring and helping other people understand what he had learned from God's Word.

Questions for Thought:

1. Why was Martin Luther an unhappy child?
2. What did he do to try to find peace with God?
3. What did he finally come to understand?
4. How do we get forgiveness and acceptance by God?

Memory Verse: "Therefore having been justified by faith, we have peace with God through our Lord Jesus Christ" (Romans 5:1).

Tiny Tot Verse: "Peace with God through our Lord Jesus Christ" (Romans 5:1).

NATURE CORNER: SHADOWS

"What goes through fire and does not burn, through water and does not drown, or walks through straw and does not rustle?" The answer to this Lithuanian riddle is—your shadow.

When people are very timid we say they are afraid even of their own shadow. Early in the morning and late in the afternoon your shadow becomes very big like a giant. If you didn't know better, you might be afraid of it. At noon when the sun is high in the sky your shadow is very tiny.

Some people who live near the equator won't go outside at noon because their shadow is so small at that time of day. They get the feeling that they too are shrinking and beginning to disappear.

Many people are superstitious about their shadows. They are afraid to let it fall upon an open grave lest they be the next one to die. Some people believe that the shadow is a person's soul. They believe they can get rid of an enemy by stabbing his shadow.

Shadows are really not so mysterious. They are simply dark images cast upon a surface by something that gets in the way of light rays. A tree casts a shadow because it blocks a little bit of the sun's rays. You cast a shadow when you stand in front of a light.

When too much sunlight enters your house, you pull a window shade or drape to make shade. Shade is a shadow. We find shade outdoors too, under trees and next to buildings that block the sun's rays. Shade feels good when the sun gets too hot for us.

Everything has a shadow, but only when there is light present. Nighttime is simply a big shadow caused when the earth turns away from the sun. The earth casts a shadow too, but we cannot see it except when it falls on the moon. Then it prevents the moon from reflecting the rays of the sun. This is called a lunar eclipse. The moon has no light of its own, so it is dark when the earth's shadow completely blocks out the sun's light.

Sometimes on a nice day the sun suddenly disappears from view. We feel that the sun has left us, but it really hasn't. The sun is still there in the sky, but we cannot see it because clouds have hidden it from our view. On rainy days the sun can be hidden by clouds all day long, but the sun is not gone.

Jesus is our sun. He gives us spiritual light and warms us with His love. Troubles are like clouds that hide the sun. When things go wrong it seems that our sun, the Lord Jesus, has left us. But that is not true. He is there even though hard things are hiding Him from us.

David realized that even though he walked through "the valley of the shadow of death" he need not fear because the Lord was with him. If we have put our trust in Him we can be sure He is with us too. We don't need to fear either little or big shadows.

Questions for Thought:

1. How are shadows made?
2. What kind of shadows do you like?
3. What is the biggest shadow of all?

4. How are troubles like shadows?
5. What has Jesus promised about the "valley of the shadow?"

Memory Verse: "Even though I walk through the valley of the shadow of death, I fear no evil; for Thou art with me" (Psalm 23:4).

Tiny Tot Verse: "Thou art with me" (Psalm 23:4).

HYMN STORY: "A MIGHTY FORTRESS IS OUR GOD"

Martin Luther wrote about forty hymns. The one most remembered is his great "A Mighty Fortress Is Our God," the battle song of the Reformation. In this hymn Luther expresses man's helplessness in the face of his foes, but also how the power of Christ is greater than any enemy. So, the Christian need not fear.

Luther sang this hymn every day while staying in the Castle of Coburg. For six months he was under an imperial ban and could not attend the Diet of Augsburg, where his friends debated his beliefs and struggled for religious freedom for the newly formed Lutheran Church.

Later this song became even more appropriate when Lutherans suffered persecution—one pastor was burned alive. It is an excellent song for our times too. Learn it as a family.

A Mighty Fortress Is Our God

A mighty fortress is our God, a bulwark never failing;
Our helper He, amid the flood of mortal ills prevailing.
For still our ancient foe doth seek to work us woe;
His craft and power are great, and armed with cruel hate,
On earth is not His equal.

Did we in our own strength confide, our striving would be losing,
Were not the right Man on our side, the Man of God's own choosing.
Dost ask who that may be? Christ Jesus, it is He;
Lord Sabaoth His name, from age to age the same,
And He must win the battle.

And though this world, with devils filled, should threaten to undo us,
We will not fear, for God hath willed His truth to triumph through us.
The prince of darkness grim,—we tremble not for him;
His rage we can endure, for lo! his doom is sure,
One little word shall fell him.

That word above all earthly powers—no thanks to them—abideth;
The Spirit and the gifts are ours through Him who with us sideth.
Let goods and kindred go, this mortal life also;
The body they may kill: God's truth abideth still,
His kingdom is forever.

Through this song you can teach your children the following truths:

1. God is our fortress and helper.
2. He never fails us.
3. Jesus is on our side.
4. Satan is our strong foe, but God is stronger.
5. We can't win in our own strength.
6. Jesus wins the battle for us when we trust Him.
7. We need not fear.
8. God's truth will triumph.
9. We conquer through His Word.
10. His kingdom is forever.

Memory Verse: "But thanks be to God, who gives us the victory through our Lord Jesus Christ" (1 Corinthians 15:57).

Tiny Tot Verse: "Victory through our Lord Jesus Christ" (1 Corinthians 15:57).

ACTIVITIES

Pantomime

Have children pantomime the actions of Martin Luther while one of the parents reviews the reformer's story. Let them perform being struck by lightning, reading the Bible; climbing up Pilate's staircase on their knees, suddenly understanding the truth of the gospel, writing the Ninety-five Theses and nailing it to the chapel door; being kidnapped on their way to Wittenberg, galloping off on a horse to the Wartburg Castle, dressing as a knight, and translating the Bible.

Make a Horse for Martin Luther

Take a medium-sized paper bag. Cut two eyes from white and black construction paper, and paste one on each side of the bag. Draw in eyelashes with a black felt pen. Make two large ears, and staple them on top to flap over each side. Cut off the bottom of another paper bag, and cut it in strips to within one half inch of the fold to make a mane. Staple the mane so that it falls on each side. Stuff the bottom third of the bag with paper. Insert a broom handle, and your horse is ready to ride.

Rake Leaves

This would be fun to do before dinner with the promise of a Family Night that includes a story and treats. If time permits, play table games such as Uno, Sorry, Scrabble, Monopoly, or Dominoes.

Nature Hike

Go on a hike together and collect a variety of leaves. Press some of them for future craft activities. Press them inside a book and add extra weight by stacking more books on top. A nature hike at night is the most fun of all. Choose a clear, starlit night. If you can go into a woods you might hear an owl hooting or see a beaver at work building a dam.

To see in a creek or river at night, put a flashlight in a glass jar and screw the top on tightly. Tie a string around the neck of the jar and lower it into the water to see frogs, fish, and insects.

Your discoveries may lead to a trip to the library to do further research on the interesting creatures you have found.

Halloween Party

Many parents are reluctant these days to let their children go "trick-or-treating" because of the danger involved. If you feel this way, how about letting your children plan their own special Halloween party for their friends? The children can send invitations, plan and help prepare the food, and decide on the games. If they need some help with games, you might suggest the following:

Bobbing for Apples. This must be done on a cement or linoleum floor to allow for spills. Players must keep their hands behind their backs and get hold of the apple with their teeth. Those who do so may eat their apples. As a variation, tie apples on strings and let the children try to get a bite of them without using their hands.

Pin on the Grin. Instead of the traditional tail on the donkey, why not use a large picture of a jack-o-lantern and see who can get the closest to putting its grin where it belongs? Don't forget the blindfold.

Dress-up Relay. Divide the children into two teams of equal number. Put an identical outfit of clothes in two suitcases. Each child must run to the suitcase, put on the clothes, take them off, put them back in the suitcase, and run to the end of the line. The next child then takes his turn. The team that finishes first wins. Be sure to include baggy trousers, big shoes, and a funny hat.

A Visit to Uncle George. This is a scary game, and children love to be scared on Halloween night. An adult or teenager dressed like a man lies on a bed with his head at the foot and men's shoes on his hands. His head is covered with a blanket; only the shoes stick out. Put a mask over the person's feet and top them with a man's hat.

A guide brings each child in separately to see Uncle George who is supposedly ill. A dim light adds to the eeriness. The guide takes the child to Uncle George's head—actually his feet—and talks about what a good man he is and how sick he is. Suddenly, in the midst of the conversation, Uncle George sits up and yells.

The child is startled to see the head coming from the foot of the bed and will probably scream. This adds to the suspense of the children who are waiting for their turn to see Uncle George. What caused the scream? Uncle George then settles back into bed for his next visitor.

SOURCES

Leonard W. Cowie, *Martin Luther* (New York: Frederick A. Praeger, 1966).

R. Gardner and D. Webster, *Shadow Science* (New York: Doubleday, 1976).

H.V. Harper, *Profiles of Protestant Saints* (New York: Fleet Press Corp., 1968).

Maria Leach, *The Soup Stone* (Parsippany: Funk and Wagnalls, 1954).

Mary McNeer and Lynd Ward, *Martin Luther* (New York: Abingdon Press, 1953).

Lillie Patterson, *Halloween* (Westport: Garrard Publishing Co., 1963).

11

November

November was the ninth month in the old calendar before Julius Caesar revised it. So November in Latin does not mean eleven but nine.

November is an exciting month in some parts of the world. The English celebrate Guy Fawkes Day on November 5, complete with huge bonfires and firecrackers. In Thailand people honor the god of the waterways in November, sending lighted candles floating down the river in small boats made from banana leaves and lotus petals. Besides this celebration the Thais enjoy an elephant round-up festival every November. Streets are closed to traffic for elephant riding, elephant racing, and even an elephant tug-of-war—one elephant against 100 men.

Our November has two important holidays: Thanksgiving and Armistice Day. Rather than a time of exuberant celebration, these holidays lend themselves to quiet periods of reflection. We thank God for the peace and freedom our brave forefathers fought so hard to win for us. We thank Him for the Pilgrims who braved extreme hardships to seek out a place where people could worship God as they pleased. We thank Him, too, for the brave men who fought to preserve this and other freedoms for us.

When the Pilgrims reaped their first harvest, they celebrated with a thanksgiving feast to the Lord, sharing their bounty with their Indian friends. Wild fowl, venison, fish, clams, oysters, lobster, eel, and vegetables the early settlers raised with the Indians' help graced the tables that first Thanksgiving.

The Pilgrims could have found reason to grumble after suffering through that first winter and losing so many of their number. Instead, they were grateful to be alive, grateful for a harvest, grateful for a land where they could worship God as they pleased. Let us follow them in their attitude of gratitude.

ESPECIALLY FOR PARENTS

My thanksgiving used to be hit and miss, mostly miss, I'm afraid. I found more things to grumble about than to be grateful for. Negative attitudes overtook my life until I suffered a nervous breakdown followed by months of deep depression.

One evening God showed me that I should be thanking Him instead of feeling sorry for myself—I should be grateful instead of grumbling. Had He not forgiven my sins, given me eternal life? Had He not promised to be with me every day and give me strength for each trial? Was He not in control of every situation of my life and working all things together for my good?

As an attitude of gratitude replaced my grumbling and became a way of life for me, my self-pity, discontent, and negative thoughts had to retreat. My depression was replaced with the joy of living, my aimlessness with purpose. I learned to thank God for the little commonplace things I had taken for granted so long: the sunlight coming in my window, clean sheets for my bed, the strength to bake a batch of cookies. I learned to deeply appreciate the treasures God had given me: salvation, His Word, His unfailing presence, my husband and family. I began to learn to thank Him even for the difficulties and frustrations of my life, believing the promise "All things work together for good to them that love God" (Romans 8:28). My life changed dramatically when I adopted an attitude of gratitude.

An old plaque used to grace the walls of many Christian homes:

> Christ is the unseen Guest at every meal,
> The silent Listener to every conversation.

I wonder how often our unseen Guest and silent Listener hears words of grumbling in our homes? Do we as parents promote such a spirit by our griping? Do we concentrate on the negative, look on the dark side of every situation, spread gloom about us? If so, we are inadvertently turning our children into pessimistic, negative individuals, teaching them to be grouchy instead of grateful.

George Beverly Shea, the well-known gospel singer, tells us in his story, *Songs That Lift the Heart,* that he woke up every morning to his mother's cheerful singing. What an influence that had on his life!

Some of us can't sing well enough to do that, but we can hum a cheery tune. We can smile, we can serve positive, happy remarks with the cereal for breakfast to help our children adopt a positive attitude for the day.

As a newscaster was talking about a great football team he said, "Their greatest asset is their attitude." I was expecting him to say something about their size, skill, or strategy. No, it was their attitude that made them winners.

One of the greatest gifts we can give our children is an attitude of thanksgiving—the ability to make the best of every situation and to see God's hand in their lives working all things together for good.

We are told in Psalm 22:3 that God inhabits the praises of His people. When we praise God we are permitting Him to come into our circumstances and work out something beautiful for us.

I hope you won't wait as long as I did to adopt an attitude of gratitude. I hope you'll not delay to pass this attitude on to your children. Remember, attitudes are caught more readily than taught. Teaching your children to be grateful to God must be supplemented by your own example of a grateful attitude.

FAMILY DEVOTIONS

BIBLE STUDY: THE ISRAELITES GRUMBLE

The Israelites were leaving Egypt. How excited the children must have been as they started off in the middle of the night away from the land of slavery to a land of freedom. But how frightened they became a few days later when they saw Pharaoh's army coming after them to force them back into slavery in Egypt. The king had changed his mind about letting them go.

(Read or tell the story from Exodus 14:1-28 of the miraculous deliverance from Pharaoh's forces as God opened up the Red Sea for the Israelites' escape and their enemies' destruction. Talk about their happiness as recorded in Exodus 15.)

Just as Israel was saved from Pharaoh and the slavery of Egypt, Jesus saves us from the slavery of the devil and the power of sin when we believe in Him. We should be thankful to know we are forgiven and have eternal life.

But what happened to the Israelites? Did they stay thankful? No, as soon as they ran into a problem they began to grumble (Exodus 14:22-25). God provided water for them to drink, but they grumbled again (Exodus 16:2-3). God provided manna for them, a food He spread out on the ground like dew every morning, but still the people grumbled. Exodus 17:2 states that they complained because there was no water. Later they complained because they were tired of the food God provided for them (Numbers 11:4-6). They grumbled and grumbled. Let's see what God thought of their attitude.

1. Exodus 16:7. He hears our grumbling. (Talk about grumbling in your home.)

2. Exodus 16:7. Our grumblings are against Him. Why does the Bible say that? (He arranges our circumstances.)

3. Numbers 11:1. God is displeased with our grumbling. Why? (Discuss how much God had done for the Israelites—opened the Red Sea, etc.—and how much He has done for us, saved us from sin, promised us heaven, etc.) Instead of our grumbling, God wants our gratitude.

Read and discuss the following verses about giving thanks:

Psalm 34:1—at all times
Psalm 79:13—forever
Psalm 107:1—because the Lord is good
Psalm 138:1—with all my heart
Ephesians 5:20—for all things

Stress that the Lord does what is best for us, so we should thank Him even when we don't understand why things happen the way they do. Someday we will understand. Encourage each family member to pray a prayer of thanksgiving, listing several things for which he is grateful.

Memory Verse: "In everything give thanks; for this is God's will for you in Christ Jesus" (1 Thessalonians 5:18).

Tiny Tot Verse: "In everything give thanks" (1 Thessalonians 5:18).

A HERO TO FOLLOW: MANUEL'S CHOICE

Manuel shivered as he began to hoe the corn on the steep mountainside.* It was chilly in the mornings, but soon the sun would come out, and then it would be too warm. He sighed as he swung his hoe. If only he were in school instead of out in the field hoeing. But Father had insisted that he quit school and learn to work like a man.

For a moment Manuel forgot to work. He leaned on his hoe, looking down into the valley and at the mountains beyond. What mysterious, exciting wonders lay behind those mountains? He had learned about some of them when he went to school, but now his school days were over.

"Someday," Manuel promised himself, "I will leave my village and see the wonders of the outside world. Someday I will go to school again."

The Indian boy was about to continue his hoeing when a movement in the valley below caught his eye. Some people were coming up the trail to the village. He watched, entranced, as the procession came closer. Then his eyes widened in surprise. One of the men climbing the mountain trail was not an Indian like Manuel. Nor was he a Mexican like the people who owned the big houses in the valley. He was tall, skinny, and as pale as death! Manuel dropped his hoe and ran to tell his father.

All the people in the village of Zapotillan were curious of the stranger from the United States, but none more so than Manuel. The adults kept an aloof distance, but the young people crowded around the foreigner and watched everything he did.

He was especially interesting to observe after he brought his young wife to the village. Excitedly Manuel reported what he had seen through the windows of the American's house. "The senora stands when she cooks. Then she sits and eats right with her husband. They always close their eyes before they eat food."

Gradually Manuel discovered other things about the foreigner who had come to live in their village. He didn't get drunk or beat his wife and was kind to everyone. He had come to Zapotillan to teach the people about his God. In order to do that he had to learn the language of the Totonac Indians.

Manuel was thrilled when the American teacher asked him to help

* Adapted from *Challenge*, Regular Baptist Press. Used by permission.

with the language study. "I must put the words of God's Book into the language of your people," he explained.

At first Manuel thought the teacher was strange to believe in a God he could not see. Manuel could *see* his gods. Six wooden gods sat solemnly on a low shelf in his home. Every day Mother gathered her family to pray to them. How foolish the missionary was to pray to a God he couldn't see, mused Manuel.

As Manuel helped the teacher put the words of the Bible into the Totonac tongue, he began to wonder about the six wooden gods on the shelf in his home. Were they real gods, or was the teacher's God the true One? If only he could know for sure.

One day Manuel decided to find out. While his mother was busy pounding the corn for tortilla, Manuel searched in her sewing basket for a long needle. His heart pounding furiously and looking nervously behind him to make sure no one was watching, he moved toward the gods with the long needle. His mouth felt dry when he realized what he was about to do—stick the needle into the foot of one of the gods. If the foot bled, Manuel would know the god was alive and would believe on him and the other five gods as well. If the foot didn't bleed, Manuel would know the god was only a wooden idol and believe on the teacher's God.

Taking a deep breath, Manuel thrust the needle into the foot of one of the gods on the dusty shelf. The needle broke. The foot did not bleed.

Manuel ran to his mother and told her what he had done. "They are not gods, Mother," he said, "only idols. The teacher's God is the true One. I will follow Him."

Mother became very upset and frightened. She wrung her hands in despair. "You have insulted the gods," she cried, "and will die in thirty minutes."

Manuel couldn't help but feel afraid as he ran to the missionary's house to tell him about it. Would he die as Mother had said?

The missionary was glad to see Manuel and explained that whoever believed on God's Son would receive eternal life.

Manuel had heard the story before, but never really understood it. Suddenly he realized that the teacher's God was a real Person. Manuel could not see Him but he could believe in Him. How happy he became as he realized that the true God had given him eternal life. Excitedly he ran home to tell his mother.

"See, I did not die," he told her. "Instead, I have received life."

Manuel did not pray to the wooden gods after that. This made his mother fearful and his father angry. One day his father said, "Manuel, because you have forsaken the gods the whole village is in trouble. We have too much rain, and the corn is rotting in the ground. It is all your fault. We will have thunderstorms because the gods are angry, and all our cornfields will be washed away. The evil spirits will suck the life from the little children. You must give up this new God that you have taken."

"I cannot do that," protested Manuel. "He has given me eternal life."

Father was very angry. "I'll give you thirty minutes to decide. Either you come back to the gods of your family or you leave this house, never to return!"

Manuel's footsteps lagged as he made his way to the teacher's house. He knew his father meant what he said. Manuel had to choose between his new God and his family. What a hard decision to make.

Before he reached the teacher's house, Manuel had made up his mind. He could never give up the true God and eternal life. He would follow Him even if it meant losing his home.

The missionary looked grave when Manuel told him what had happened. "You may live with us," he said, "and continue to help me translate the Bible into the language of your people."

Manuel stayed and helped the teacher for a whole year. He found out that "All things work together for good to them that love God." One day he got a job with a missionary in Mexico City, where he could go to school. His dream to see the outside world and get an education came true as he followed the true God.

Later, after attending schools in Mexico, Canada, the United States, and Germany and learning six languages besides Totonac, Manuel returned to his own people to start a school for them. Not only does he teach his people how to read and write their own language, but he also teaches them of the true God and His Son, Jesus Christ. He teaches God's Book to the Indians.

Manuel found out that it is not always easy to follow God's path, but it always turns out for the best in the end. How glad he was that he chose Him!

Questions for Thought:

1. What did Manuel long for?
2. What did he think was strange about the missionary?

3. How did he test the wooden gods?
4. What did his father do when he forsook the family gods?
5. Tell about the happy ending to Manuel's story.

Memory Verse: "And we know that God causes all things to work together for good to those who love God, to those who are called according to His purpose" (Romans 8:28).

Tiny Tot Verse: "God causes all things to work together for good" (Romans 8:28).

CURIOSITY CORNER: COUNTING AND SUCH

In ancient times, the use of numbers was limited because the zero had not been discovered.* The Egyptians, Romans, Chinese, and Japanese had no symbol for *nothing*. Not until zero was discovered by the Hindus of India did it become possible to multiply and use decimals.

During Medieval times, arithmetic was considered "black magic" by the clergy. How could the science of numbers be good when it was advanced by the pagan Greeks and Saracens? Those Arabic numerals by which they measured unknown mysteries had to be diabolic symbols. When a scholar wrote a book on geometry, he was accused of dabbling in black magic.

Finally a brave teacher named Rabanus Maurus decided that numbers couldn't be bad, because Jesus had said the very hairs of our heads are numbered. Maurus began to teach his pupils arithmetic. Gradually, the science of counting and measuring by numbers was accepted as not wicked after all.

Today mathematicians can study extremely large numbers. A one with a hundred zeros after it is called a googol. A googolplex is the name for a one with a googol of zeros after it. This number is so huge that a person could spend his whole lifetime counting and never get to the end of it. It reminds us of the symbol for infinity, or numbers that go on forever.

David didn't know about googols or googolplexes, but he realized there were things that could not be counted. He said in Psalm 40:5, "Many, O Lord my God, are thy wonderful works which thou hast done, and thy thoughts are to usward; they cannot be reckoned up in

---

* Adapted from *Discovery*, Light and Life Press. Used by permission.

order unto thee: if I would declare and speak of them, they are more than can be numbered" (KJV).

In Psalm 17:15 the psalmist says: "I cannot count the times you have faithfully rescued me from danger" (*The Living Bible*).

David also says of God's thoughts toward us: "If I should count them, they are more in number than the sand" (Psalm 139:18).

In modern-day language we could call God's thoughts for us a googolplex. If we ever feel alone or forsaken we had better start counting. It isn't bad to count, you know. It was only in the Dark Ages that they thought so.

Questions for Thought:

1. Who discovered the zero?
2. What did people in Medieval times think of arithmetic?
3. Why did the teacher Rabanus Maurus decide numbers couldn't be bad?
4. How long would it take a person to count a googolplex?
5. How long does it take us to count our blessings?

Let family members list or tell all the blessings they can think of. Thank God for them together.

Memory Verse: "Bless the Lord, O my soul, and forget none of His benefits" (Psalm 103:2).

Tiny Tot Verse: "Give thanks to the Lord" (Psalm 92:1).

HYMN STORY: "DOXOLOGY"

What better song is there to sing during the month of November than the Doxology? This song was taken from Psalm 134. For many years the words of the psalm were sung instead of the words we sing today.

Historians tell us that our forefathers on the Mayflower sank to their knees and sang the Doxology when after sixty-seven days at sea a lookout sighted land.

Seventeen years later Bishop Thomas Ken wrote the words to the Doxology that we sing today. It is interesting to note that this man suffered a great deal during his lifetime. He went through the great

London fire when four-fifths of the city was destroyed. He also suffered through the horrors of the bubonic plague that killed thousands.

In spite of a stormy life with many hardships, Bishop Thomas Ken maintained an attitude of praise to God, as is evidenced by this song he wrote.

> Praise God from Whom all blessings flow!
> Praise Him, all creatures, here below!
> Praise Him above, ye heavenly host!
> Praise Father, Son and Holy Ghost!

Try writing a simple hymn together as a family to the tune of the Doxology. This would be a good activity for Thanksgiving Day. Here is an example—you can do better.

> Praise God for parents, Mom and Dad!
> Praise Him for all that makes us glad!
> Praise Him for children, big and small!
> Praise Him for Jesus, best of all!

Or write a simple praise song to the tune of "Jesus Loves Me." Other praise songs might include "Count Your Blessings," "Praise Him All Ye Little Children," and "Alleluia."

Memory Verse: "I will bless the Lord at all times; His praise shall continually be in my mouth" (Psalm 34:1).

Tiny Tot Verse: "Praise the Lord" (Psalm 112:1).

ACTIVITIES

Scrapbooks

Make scrapbooks of things for which you are thankful. Provide a scrapbook or paper that can be folded together and stapled or tied with yarn. Use old magazines, catalogs, and greeting cards. Children can write in appropriate Thanksgiving verses from the Psalms such as 103:2; 107:1; 111:1; 116:17.

Encourage them to think of a title to write on their construction paper cover with crayons or felt-tipped pens. Or buy tagboard and give each child a piece with which to make a Thanksgiving poster to hang in his room.

This activity needs only a minimum of preparation but could be of maximum value to your child as he learns to count his blessings in this tangible way.

Games

Musical Chairs. Put chairs back to back in the middle of a room, one fewer than the number of players. Play a music box, record, or piano while the players march around the chairs. When the music stops, players scramble for seats. The one left without a seat drops out of the game, removing a chair as he leaves. The one who gets the last seat wins.

Category Game. Dad starts by calling out a category, pointing at a family member, and counting to ten. The one pointed at must give an answer from the category before the number ten is reached. If he doesn't, he becomes "It" and must choose the next category. Allow categories to be repeated but not items in the categories. Suggested categories: cars and other vehicles, vegetables, fruits, animals, sports, countries, continents, rivers, people, colors, books, songs.

Feeding the Birds

When the snow begins to fall, the birds have a harder time finding food. Children will enjoy the fun of helping and watching them.

Insect-eating birds like suet, or pieces of fat from your meat. Press suet into a pine cone and hang up in a tree where a dog can't get it, or press the fat into the bark of the tree. Bluebirds, chickadees, and bluejays will appreciate your efforts.

Seed-eating birds such as sparrows, cardinals, and bobwhites would like birdseed put on a small wooden shelf with a little edge on it, so that the seed won't fall off. Nail on a porch, a post, or a tree.

Hummingbirds are satisfied with red-colored sugar water put in a hummingbird feeder or in a pill bottle wired to a bush.

Make Christmas Gifts

November is the time to start making Christmas gifts. Prime your child's imagination. How about a jigsaw puzzle for his cousin? A placemat for Grandma?

Jigsaw Puzzle. Glue a picture on cardboard. Draw the pieces on the back and make them all different if possible. Cut out and put into a box for an original, handmade Christmas gift.

Placemat. Use the leaves you collected on a nature hike for a lovely placemat. Mount on a heavy piece of paper. Cover with transparent contact paper to make your placemat waterproof and durable.

Crayon or paint messages on paper and decorate with small pictures to make a placemat for a very special person. Messages could include: I Love You, You Are Special, The World's Best Mom, Dad's Number One!, or Grandma's Place. Cover the mat with transparent contact paper.

Make a design by folding a piece of paper twice. Randomly cut out a few notches. Fold again, cut again, fold again, and cut. Open up to see a beautiful design that can be placed on a sheet of construction paper or tagboard and covered on both sides with transparent contact paper to make a lovely placemat. Or cut out a snowflake design by cutting a piece of paper into a circle, or cut around a plate. Fold paper in half, then in half again. Fold twice more, then cut notches and corners. Open it up and find your snowflake.

Pine Cone Plaques or Wreaths. Collect pine cones and glue them on a circular piece of cardboard to make a lovely wreath. This can be spray painted or left in its natural color. Make attractive plaques by gluing small pine cones on pieces of sanded board. Print Bible verses or other wise sayings underneath.

Decoupaged Plaques. Save cute pictures from magazines, greeting cards, and calendars. Teach your children to make attractive plaques by pasting the articles on small boards. The boards must be sanded until smooth, then covered with a layer of Fun Podge or white glue thinned with a couple of drops of water. Put the picture on the board and smooth out, then brush on more Fun Podge or glue and let dry before repeating the process. Diamond dust purchased at the hobby store can be sprinkled on after the last application of glue to make your project sparkle. Fasten a picture hook on for hanging.

Dried Flower Plaques. Did your children press favorite flowers during the summer and fall? These will make lovely plaques or bookmarks, especially if mounted on dark velvet material. Enclose in transparent contact paper.

Fun with Old Jeans. Can you find two matching square or oblong pieces in a pair of old jeans? Then let your child make a bag for a family member. Tack the pieces together on three sides with the right sides facing in. Then turn right side out and blanket-stitch around the edges with bright yarn. Braid a yarn handle and fasten.

Winter Bouquet. Collect winter weeds, dry, and put in a vase. Or gather weeds (milkweed, yarrow, cattails, heather, goldenrod, wild mustard) and let dry. Spray them with fixative from an art store to preserve them. Or dip in colored paint and let them dry. It makes a lovely gift for Mom.

An Original Game

Provide Bobby with a board or heavy piece of cardboard, paints, glue, old buttons, and old magazines, and let him figure out an original game for a family member or friend. You may be surprised at his ingenuity. Or give him shoe boxes to make a train for little brother, using string to join the boxes together for pulling. Draw windows on the sides and letter on the name of the train.

SOURCES

Albert Edward Bailey, *The Gospel in Hymns* (New York: Charles Scribner's Sons, 1956).

Deluxe Appointment Book (New York: Bobley Publishing Corp., 1980).

Patricia Lauber, *The Story of Numbers* (E.M. Hale and Co., 1961).

Winifred Trask Lee, *A Forest of Pencils* (New York: Bobbs-Merrill Co., 1961).

Hugh Stevens, *Manuel* (Miami: Editorial Caribe, 1981).

12

December

December, meaning "tenth month" in Latin, was the tenth month of the year before the calendar was changed. Now it is the last. It is an exciting month because it contains Christmas, the celebration of the birth of our Savior. It can also be the most hectic month of the year if we aren't careful.

Did you know that Jesus' birthday was not celebrated on December 25 until the fourth century A.D., over 300 years after Jesus was born? Nobody is sure just what time of the year Jesus was born. Some early Christians celebrated His birthday in the spring, while others celebrated it in the winter.

The people of the Roman Empire worshiped the sun. They felt lonely and sad when winter came and the days began to get shorter. They were afraid their god, the sun, would go away and never come back.

When the days began to grow longer in late December, the people were happy. They believed their god was coming back to warm the earth and make their crops grow. They honored the sun god with lighted candles, lamps, and bonfires on December 25.

When the early Christians were trying to decide on a day for the celebration of Jesus' birthday, someone suggested December 25. It was already a Roman holiday. The people who worshiped the sun could celebrate to their god, but the Christians would celebrate the birth of their Savior. The church leaders hoped this would keep the Christians from taking part in the pagan festivities.

As Christianity spread over Europe, many people became Christians. They celebrated Christ's birth on December 25. However, they brought some of their pagan customs into the celebration of Christmas.

Candles, evergreens, mistletoe, carols, feasting, and other customs that are now part of our Christmas were borrowed from the pagan festival to the sun.

Interestingly, Santa Claus had a Christian origin but now seems to have nothing to do with the true meaning of Christmas. In the fourth century A.D., a young boy named Nicholas lost both his parents but inherited a great deal of money. Because Nicholas loved God and the poor, he used all of his wealth to help others. He always gave his gifts in secret. Many legends rose up about this kind, generous man. After he died, people honored Saint Nicholas on December 6, which was his feast day.

Gradually, through the years Saint Nicholas became a legend which evolved into our modern Santa Claus—the fat jolly man with a white beard who lives at the North Pole and brings gifts to good boys and girls at Christmas. Unfortunately, Santa Claus has taken the place of Jesus in the Christmas celebration of many boys and girls.

Did you know that at one time the celebration of Christmas was forbidden? When the Puritans took over England in the 1600s they felt that Christmas had become too worldly. They disliked the pagan customs that had become a part of it. Town criers were sent through the streets crying, "No Christmas! No Christmas!" On December 25 everyone had to go to work as usual. Nobody could sing carols, have programs, or celebrate. Of course some people disobeyed the law and celebrated in secret.

When the Puritans reached the New World they brought with them these stern practices. It was against the law in early New England to celebrate Christmas or attend a Christmas service on Christmas Day. As late as 1870 children were required to attend school in New England on Christmas Day.

Settlers from other lands—the Germans, Dutch, and Irish—however, continued to celebrate Christmas in America as they had in their homelands. Gradually the other settlers were won over, and Christmas became a celebration for all Americans.

Today many people in our country and in other countries of the world celebrate Christmas with no regard for its original meaning.

They could just as well be celebrating the sun's return as people did in ancient times.

We honor the Son of God who came to bring eternal light to people on earth. Let's be sure to keep Him in our Christmas celebrations.

ESPECIALLY FOR PARENTS

What are your family Christmas traditions? Oyster stew on Christmas Eve or a Christmas Day breakfast? We serve Japanese food—sukiyaki—on Christmas Eve. It became a family favorite while we were living in Japan. We always have turkey with all the trimmings on Christmas Day.

Our parents served Norwegian dishes on Christmas Eve. On Christmas morning the familiar, and disliked, oatmeal was missing and in its place were Christmas breads, *lefse*, and oranges. When I was a child, we seldom had oranges except at Christmas. The smell of oranges still fills me with nostalgia, taking me back to Christmases of long ago.

We found that as our boys were growing up they wanted to celebrate Christmas in the same way every year. They liked changes, but not when it came to celebrating holidays—they wanted to keep the family traditions. Without the familiar events it didn't seem like Christmas.

Young couples just starting their families may not yet have their own family Christmas traditions. If their parents live nearby they no doubt simply go home for Christmas. This is a happy arrangement, but there comes a time when young families need to establish their own Christmas traditions. Remember, the way you start is likely the way you will continue, as your children will want to do the same familiar things each year.

What will you eat? Where will you go? When will you open your gifts? Whom will you invite? How will you decorate? Why not give your folks a break and invite them over for the Christmas celebration at your house for a change?

One family I know buys a special Christmas decoration for each child every year to hang on the Christmas tree. When the child leaves home to establish a home of his own, the decorations go with him.

More important than the outward trappings are the spiritual traditions you establish. Work to honor Christ in your Christmas. This will be the invaluable tradition your children will never forget.

Keep Christ in Christmas

A journalist interviewed a number of celebrities in our country to find out what made their Christmas meaningful. Most of them talked about family get-togethers, Christmas feasts, and gift-giving. None mentioned the One whose birthday we remember at Christmas.

Secular Christmas songs are replacing many of the old familiar carols. When you go Christmas shopping in December, you will probably hear "Rudolph, the Red-nosed Reindeer" more often than "Silent Night."

It is easy to get caught up in the externals of Christmas: shopping and wrapping gifts, baking Christmas goodies, decorating the house. Often Christ is left out or at least pushed off into the corner.

We don't want to be like Scrooge and frown on the festivities of Christmas. We certainly don't want to ban the celebration of Christmas like the Puritans. But what can we do in the midst of all this secularism to keep Christ in the center?

1. Stress Jesus' Birth. Some Christian families try to keep Christ in their Christmas by making a birthday cake for Him complete with candles to blow out. Explain that Jesus' birth in Bethlehem was not His beginning but only His beginning as a man. He existed from eternity with the Father as the eternal Son of God.

Other Christian families make advent wreaths with five candles. *Advent* means "coming" and is traditionally a time to prepare one's heart for Christmas. A family member lights a candle each week beginning the first week of December. It burns while the family has a time of thanksgiving and prayer for the coming of Jesus. The second week two candles will be lit, until Christmas Eve when all five candles will burn in celebration of the Light of the world whose birth we celebrate.

2. Emphasize Giving. I remember a day when I was five years old and very excited. It was Daddy's birthday, the house was all cleaned up, and we were having company. One by one the guests arrived, each with a beautifully wrapped package. I couldn't wait until Daddy opened his presents.

To my dismay I discovered later in the evening that the presents weren't for Daddy after all but for my half-sister and her husband who had recently eloped. I felt puzzled and hurt. It was Daddy's birthday! Why didn't he get the presents?

Children are often puzzled about why everyone else gets presents on Jesus' birthday. It is important to explain how they can give to Him. In Proverbs 23:26 we read, "Give me your heart, my son." Explain that

Jesus doesn't want a store-bought gift but simply our love, devotion, and worship. He also wants our gratitude and praises. Have special times beside the Christmas tree with your children to praise and worship Jesus. An appropriate song to learn is, "Jesus, We Just Want to Thank You."

In Matthew 25:40 Jesus says that when we do something for others we are doing it for Him. He also tells us not to entertain only those who can entertain us back but also the poor, lonely, and disabled.

Discuss with your children what needy person you can invite over for a dinner or an evening. Perhaps you know a lonely widow or bachelor, a newly-divorced person and his or her children, a refugee family, an exchange student from another country, or a serviceman who can't go home for Christmas, who needs love and attention.

Sharing your Christmas gifts and feasting with them would be a beautiful way to give Jesus a Christmas gift. If that is not feasible, how about inviting them over a day or two before or after Christmas?

3. Sing Christmas Carols. Teach your children several Christmas carols each year. Sing them while sitting by your lighted tree, or follow the Scandinavian custom of singing them while walking around the Christmas tree. Play Christmas music on your stereo or radio as you make Christmas goodies together.

FAMILY DEVOTIONS

BIBLE STUDY: IT REALLY HAPPENED!

Older children especially will be fascinated by a study of the prophecies concerning the birth, life, and death of Jesus. A study such as this will make Christmas even more meaningful to them.

Find the Old Testament prophecy first, then compare it with the New Testament account. The faith of your children will be strengthened as they see how literally those ancient prophecies were fulfilled. Explain that David lived 1000 years, Isaiah and Micah about 700, Daniel about 500, and Zechariah nearly 500 years before Christ's birth.

Micah 5:2—Matthew 2:1. The birth of Jesus.
Isaiah 35:4-6—Matthew 11:4-5. The life of Jesus.
Isaiah 53:1—Matthew 26:67-68. The rejection of Jesus.

Isaiah 53:7—Matthew 27:10-14. Jesus made no answer when accused by Jews.

Zechariah 11:12-13—Matthew 26:14-15. Jesus sold for thirty pieces of silver.

Zechariah 11:12-13—Matthew 27:3-7. The pieces of silver were used to buy a potter's field where poor people could be buried.

Psalm 22:16—Matthew 27:31. Jesus was crucified—crucifixion was unheard of when this psalm was written; the Romans invented it 800 years later.

Psalm 22:18—Matthew 27:35. They cast lots for Jesus' clothes.

Isaiah 53:12—Luke 23:34. Jesus prayed for His enemies.

Isaiah 53:23—Matthew 27:38. Jesus died with criminals.

Isaiah 53:9—Matthew 27:57-60. Jesus was buried with the rich.

Daniel 2:44—2 Peter 3:9-13; Revelation 22:20. Jesus will return.

Talk about the certainty of Christ's second coming to take His children to heaven and then to establish His kingdom on earth.

A HERO TO FOLLOW: THE POOR MAN'S FRIEND

William Booth came home to his family after conducting a Christmas service in the Salvation Army Hall in Whitechapel. His wife had prepared a delicious Christmas dinner. As the parents and six children gathered around the table they thanked God for His gifts to them.

But Booth could not enjoy his Christmas dinner or the frolicking with his children that followed. He kept thinking about the homeless men and women and neglected children that he had seen on the streets that morning on his way home. They were not having a happy Christmas!

Suddenly he cried out to his wife, "I'll never spend a Christmas Day like this again! The poor have nothing but the public house!" Mr. Booth began at once to make plans for the following Christmas. He would see to it that the needy had a hot Christmas dinner before he sat down to enjoy his own.

Sure enough, the next Christmas William Booth and his family distributed 300 hot Christmas meals to the poor. Who can count the number of Christmas meals served to the needy by the Salvation Army since that time?

Yes, William Booth started an army, an army dedicated to caring for the physical needs of men, women, and children while seeking to win them to the Savior.

William Booth was born in Nottingham, England, in 1829. When he was only thirteen years old his father lost all of his money, so William had to go to work. He became an apprentice in a pawn shop. People who needed money pawned their treasures. William felt sorry for them.

One day William was called home because his father was dying. "I'm leaving, Will," said his father, "you'll have to look after the family."

William felt very sober as he watched his father die. He began to worry about dying. What came after death?

"Don't worry about it, Will," said his mother. "If you're a good boy, all will be well."

Young Booth wasn't satisfied with that answer. At his first opportunity he went to a chapel. There the preacher said, "It's not enough to try to be good. Everyone needs a Savior to take away his sin. That Savior is Jesus Christ."

He went back to the chapel again and again to hear the preacher. One day, at the age of fifteen, he knelt down and asked Christ to forgive his sins. "God, you can have all of William Booth," he said.

William began to preach on the streets after he had finished his day's work at the pawn shop. On Sundays he gathered up as many boys as he could find and brought them to church. But the people didn't want him to bring all those dirty, noisy boys into their fine church. They told him to use the back door and put the boys where nobody would see them.

"Somebody should start a church for the slum people!" declared William, who turned out to be that "somebody." Some years later, after he had married and become a preacher, he and his young wife devoted themselves to helping the poor people of the slums and winning them to Christ. He represented Christianity with its sleeves rolled up.

William Booth became the poor man's friend, and many of them were converted to Christ. William and his new believers banded together to form an army for the Lord, the Salvation Army. They used military terms—prayer was "knee-drill," taking an offering was "firing cartridges," leading a person to Jesus was "taking a prisoner," the leader was "the General," the others were "soldiers," dying was "being promoted to Glory."

Some people did not like the Salvation Army, whose members spoke out strongly against sin. Sometimes hoodlums pelted the Salvationists with potatoes, onions, eggs, and even bricks. The soldiers, who received very little pay, picked up the potatoes and onions and took them home to make stew.

The Salvation Army grew and grew until it spread all over the world. It provided lodging places for homeless people, food for the hungry, homes for orphans, and relief in time of natural disasters, such as earthquakes or floods. Most important of all, the Salvation Army brought the news of their Savior to people everywhere, and is still doing so today.

General Wiliam Booth appeared before King Edward VII of England and was asked to write in the monarch's autograph album. He wrote:

<blockquote>
Your Majesty,

Some men's ambition is art,
Some men's ambition is fame,
Some men's ambition is gold,
My ambition is the souls of men.
</blockquote>

General Booth was eighty-three years old when he "laid down his sword" and was "promoted to Glory." Queen Mary, along with thousands of his friends from the slums, attended the funeral.

Questions for Thought:

1. How did William Booth become a Christian?
2. Why couldn't he enjoy his Christmas dinner?
3. What does the Salvation Army do for people?
4. What does "promoted to Glory" mean?
5. What can you do for unfortunate people this Christmas?

Memory Verse: "Truly I say to you, to the extent that you did it to one of these brothers of Mine, even the least of them, you did it to Me" (Matthew 25:40).

Tiny Tot Verse: "You did it to Me" (Matthew 25:40).

NATURE CORNER: BRRRR

Did you know that anti-freeze was invented long before the automobile? Fish that live in polar waters where the temperature gets down to 28 or 29 degrees contain a chemical in their blood that works like anti-freeze. The fluids within these fish remain liquid even in freezing temperatures.

There is a fish in Antarctica with white blood. This strange fish has fewer red cells than other fish. Red cells carry oxygen to the tissues, but this fish doesn't need as much oxygen as red-blooded polar fish. That enables him to live under the sea ice where oxygen is scarce.

Did you know that the bodies of some insects also contain an anti-freeze substance? It is amazing to see how they adapt to cold. In some, the salts in their systems turn to sugar as cold weather approaches. Others have so little liquid in their tissues it would be difficult for them to freeze. Others, such as the potato beetle, have lots of water in their systems during the summer but dehydrate in preparation for winter. Some insects combat the cold weather by spending more time as a larva. A snug cocoon isn't a bad place to spend the winter.

Polar animals and insects are well suited to cold temperatures. Put an elephant in Antarctica and he would soon complain of a frozen trunk. Can you picture a slender flamingo standing on ice all day? Polar animals are stockier than animals in tropical regions and have smaller paws, ears, tails, and noses than their cousins in warmer places, so they are less likely to freeze. They also have a wonderful network of blood vessels at the places where their limbs join their bodies. The warm blood from their heart heats the cool blood that comes from paws or flippers resting on ice so that the cold blood does not shock their hearts, and their paws or flippers do not freeze.

Polar animals also have a heavier pelt than animals that inhabit warm places. As winter approaches that pelt grows heavier in preparation for the cold. It thins out again when spring comes. Some animals, such as polar bears and husky dogs, have a layer of fat underneath their pelts to provide added warmth.

Pigment, or the color of skin, fur, and feathers, acts as protection against the ultra-violet rays of the sun. That's why we find brilliant colors in the tropics, but mostly white or subdued colors in polar regions. Not only do the polar animals blend in with their surroundings, but their subdued color enables them to get the most benefit from the sun's rays.

Did you know that polar bears even have built-in sunglasses to combat the sun's glare on the ice and snow? Membranes over their eyes filter the sun's rays and help them focus on animals and plants.

I marvel at the wisdom of our Creator, don't you? God thought of everything! How can some people believe that all those wonders of nature "just happened"? We can see God's hand in them all.

You can see His hand in your life, too, if you think about it. Not only has He provided for your physical welfare, as He has for the polar animals, but He has also provided a Savior to forgive your sins and give you eternal life. Isn't He an amazing and wonderful God?

Questions for Thought:

1. Can you think of six ways God has enabled your body to keep warm in cold weather?
2. What most important blessing of all has God provided for you?

Memory Verse: "O Lord, how many are Thy works! In wisdom Thou has made them all" (Psalm 104:24).

Tiny Tot Verse: "Lord, how many are Thy works!" (Psalm 104:24).

HYMN STORY: "SILENT NIGHT"

Father Joseph Mohr was the priest in a village in Austria in the early 1800s. He was frustrated, because the church organ had broken down on Christmas Eve. Franz Gruber, the organist, had tried to repair it.

Mohr heaved a sigh. It was no use worrying about what he could not change. Getting to work, he started down the road to visit his parishioners. He stopped at a humble woodcutter's cottage just after a baby had been born. The kind pastor welcomed the baby before going on his way.

After making his calls, Father Mohr made his way back home. His thoughts were full of the baby he had just seen and especially of the Babe of Bethlehem, for it was Christmas Eve. As he thought about that Baby who was born the first Christmas, the words of a song came to him. When he reached home he quickly scribbled them down on a piece of paper.

Silent Night, Holy Night,
  All is calm, All is bright;
Round yon Virgin Mother and Child
  Holy Infant so tender and mild,
Sleep in heavenly peace,
  Sleep in heavenly peace.

When Father Mohr returned to the church he found that the organist had not yet been able to repair the organ. He handed him the paper on which he had scribbled the poem "Silent Night."

"Make up a tune for these words," he said, "and we will sing them as a duet for the Christmas service tomorrow accompanied by your guitar."

The organist quickly composed a tune. "It was easy," he said, "the words sang themselves."

The next day the two friends sang "Silent Night." People liked it so much they called it "Song from Heaven."

In 1863, "Stille Nacht," as it was titled in German, was translated into the beautiful English carol we sing today.

If the organ hadn't broken down on Christmas Eve in Father Mohr's church, and if a baby hadn't been born in the woodcutter's house down the road, maybe the world would not have the "Song from Heaven" recalling the silent night our Savior was born.

Memory Verse: "And she gave birth to her first-born son; and she wrapped Him in cloths, and laid Him in a manger" (Luke 2:7).

Tiny Tot Verse: "She . . . laid Him in a manger" (Luke 2:7).

ACTIVITIES

Make Christmas Tree Decorations

Strings of Popcorn and Cranberries. Probably the most familiar home-made decorations are strings of popcorn and cranberries. They make a striking decoration for the tree and are lots of fun to make with needle and thread.

Colorful Paper Chains. These can be made from last year's Christmas wrapping paper. Cut strips of paper, one inch by six inches. Paste or tape the ends together. Loop the next one through the first one and so on to make a chain to drape around the Christmas tree. Colorful construction paper can also be used.

Lid Pictures. Save your used canning lids. Glue two together with a bit of rickrack between them to make a hanger. Cut pictures from old Christmas cards and paste them on each side. Put glue on the edges and roll them in glitter from the hobby store.

For an extra special decoration, paste snapshots of the children on lids, decorate as above, and give to grandparents as a gift.

After the Christmas decorations are completed, decorate the tree together. End with a treat of hot cider and cinnamon toast.

Make Cut-Out Christmas Cookies and Decorate

Making cut-out Christmas cookies and decorating them with red and green icing was always a part of our Christmas tradition. My boys enjoyed rolling out the dough, cutting out bells, trees, and hearts with cookie cutters, taking them out of the pan with a spatula when they were baked, and decorating them with frosting. This excellent sugar cookie recipe keeps well. If preferred, you can freeze them and frost as needed.

Helen's Sugar Cookies

1 c. powdered sugar	1 1/2 t. almond flavoring
1/2 c. shortening	2 c. flour
1/2 c. margarine	1 t. cream of tartar
1 egg	1 t. soda
1 1/2 t. vanilla	1/8 t. salt

Cream sugar, shortening, and margarine. Beat in egg and flavorings. Sift dry ingredients together and add. This dough rolls better after being chilled for a few hours.

Roll out dough and cut in desired shapes. Bake in a 325 degree oven until light brown. Frost when cool with powdered sugar frosting tinted in various colors. If desired, sprinkle with candies.

You might want to double or triple this recipe so you have some cookies for treats as you make them and some to store for Christmas! To add atmosphere, play Christmas carols on your stereo while you make the cookies.

Read Together

An excellent book to start reading together as a family during the

Christmas season is *Treasures of the Snow,* by Patricia St. John. Or read *A Christmas Carol* by Charles Dickens.

Your local library no doubt has a whole shelf of Christmas books from which to choose. If your children like to read silently, make a fire in the fireplace, turn on soft Christmas music, and sit together as you read separately. Give your child a chance to share what he has read. This makes it twice as meaningful and helps him learn to express himself.

Draw a Song

You need two sides for this game, sheets of paper, and two felt tip pens. The leader tells a player from each side the name of a Christmas carol or song. The player hurries to where his teammates are waiting and tries to convey the name of the carol by drawing a picture on the paper (no words allowed). The side that guesses the song first gets a point. Then try another carol. Lots of good, creative fun!

Charades. Team One chooses a carol and reveals it to a player from Team Two. The player tries to help his team guess the carol by his actions (no words). They get five guesses before they must give up. Then Team Two chooses a carol, and a player from Team One acts it out for his team.

Pantomime

As Dad reads from Luke 2 and Matthew 2, family members pantomime the Christmas story. The innkeeper turns Mary and Joseph away, then leads them to his stable. The shepherds are first terrified by the angels, then joyfully go to Bethlehem to see Jesus. The wisemen visit Herod, then go find the new king. An angel warns Joseph to take the Baby Jesus to Egypt, away from King Herod.

Make a Creche

Let the children form the animals and figures out of clay. Make the stable and manger from popsickle sticks. Set them on a piece of wood or cardboard, and put the scene under the Christmas tree. While working, talk about the wonders of Christmas and sing carols.

SOURCES

Sallie Chesham, *Born to Battle* (Chicago: Rand-McNally, 1965).

Richard Collier, *The General Next to God* (Cleveland: Collins Publishing, 1976).

Lucy Kavaler, *Life Battles Cold* (New York: John Day, Co.).

Lillie Patterson, *Christmas Feasts and Festivals* (Champaign: Garrard Publishing Co., 1968).

Assorted Sugarfree Goodies

Spicy Bars

6 T. melted margarine
1/3 c. dark molasses
1 t. vanilla
1/8 t. salt
1/8 t. soda
1/8 t. ginger
3/4 c. chopped walnuts

3 T. honey
1 egg, slightly beaten
1 c. whole wheat flour
1 c. raisins
1/8 t. cloves
2 t. cinnamon

Add honey, molasses, egg, and vanilla to the melted margarine. Stir dry ingredients together and add to the margarine mixture. Stir in nuts and raisins. Spread onto a greased 9 x 13 inch pan. Bake 10 to 12 minutes at 375 degrees. Cut into bars and store in a covered container.

Peanut Butter Yummies

1 c. honey
3/4 c. oil
1 t. salt
3 c. quick rolled oats
2/3 c. wheat germ
1/2 c. sunflower seeds

1 beaten egg
1/4 c. water
1 t. vanilla
1 c. whole wheat flour
1/4 c. peanut butter
1 c. raisins or dates

Combine the honey, egg, water, oil, salt, and vanilla. In a separate bowl combine the dry ingredients. Add liquid mixture to dry ingredients. Add peanut butter, sunflower seeds, and raisins. Drop dough onto a greased cookie sheet. Bake at 350 degrees for 15 or 20 minutes. Make cookies large.

Granola Bars

3 1/2 c. quick oats   1 c. raisins
1 c. chopped walnuts or peanuts   2/3 c. margarine, melted
1/3 c. pure maple syrup   1/2 c. honey or molasses
1 egg, beaten   1/2 t. vanilla

Toast oats in ungreased, large, shallow baking pan in a 350 degree oven for about 15 minutes. Combine toasted oats with other ingredients. Mix well. Press into a greased 15 1/2 x 10 1/2 inch jelly roll pan. Bake for about 20 minutes at 350 degrees. Cut into bars.

Whole Wheat Pancakes

1 c. whole wheat pastry flour   1 1/4 c. buttermilk (or more)
3/4 t. soda   2 T. oil
1/4 t. baking powder   1 egg, beaten
pinch salt   dab of honey

Mix together and fry on a hot griddle, slightly greased. If you don't have whole wheat pastry flour use half whole wheat flour and half white. Variation: Make animal pancakes. It's really quite easy to spread the batter into recognizable shapes. Or make different-sized circles for head and appendages. The kids will have fun trying their hand at it.

Whole Wheat Rollups

Stir up a batch of whole wheat pancakes. Make them thin so you can spread with butter and jam or honey and roll up to eat with fingers.

Health Drops

1 c. wheat germ   2/3 c. dried milk
2/3 c. honey   1/2 c. nuts
2/3 c. peanut butter   2 T. carob powder

Mix together in a bowl and form into balls. Variation: Add rolled oats, sunflower seed nuts, raisins, or roll in toasted sesame seeds.

Fruit Tray

For a healthful treat, quarter and core 2 apples, slice 2 oranges, slice a grapefruit, or combine any fruits in season. Serve with whole wheat crackers spread with your favorite soft cheese.

Veggies and Dip

Make a dip by mixing a package of dried onion soup with a small carton of sour cream. Dip carrot sticks, celery sticks, broccoli flowerets, cauliflower, cherry tomatoes, green onions, and green peppers. Eat and enjoy. Variation: Stuff celery with cream cheese or peanut butter for a nutritious, delicious snack.

Granola

6 c. rolled oats (half quick and half old-fashioned)
1 c. sunflower seeds
1 c. shredded coconut (optional)
1 c. wheat germ or whole wheat flour
1 c. peanuts

Mix together. Add 1/2 cup honey or molasses (or mixed), 1/2 cup oil, 1/2 cup water, and 1 1/2 teaspoon vanilla. Mix well until all is coated. Put in 2 greased 9x13 inch pans and toast in oven for about 30 minutes, stirring often. When cool, add 1 cup raisins or other dried fruit. Store in the refrigerator in a covered container.

Serve as a family night snack mixed with a favorite dry cereal or alone. Add milk. Chewy and yummy! Also a good topping for ice cream.

Nuts and Bolts

Combine 2 cups each of several unsweetened cereals (puffed wheat, puffed rice, wheat biscuits, rice biscuits, corn biscuits) and 4 cups of pretzel sticks.

Melt 1/2 pound butter or margarine in a roasting pan. Add 2 tablespoons Worcestershire sauce. Stir in cereals and mix. Add 1/2 teaspoon garlic salt, 1/2 teaspoon celery salt, and 1/2 teaspoon onion salt. Add 2 cups of nutmeats. Heat in a 250 degree oven for 2 hours, stirring frequently.

Cinnamon Toast

Toast bread and spread with butter or margarine, then with honey. Sprinkle cinnamon on top and cut into four triangles or squares. Delicious with hot chocolate.

Stuffed Dates

Put a piece of nut in a pitted date and roll in powdered milk. Think of other "stuffings."

Peanut Crack

Crack peanuts in the shell for a nutritious snack.

Quickie Pizza

2 c. biscuit mix	1 can drained tomatoes
1/2 pound browned hamburger	4 t. chopped green pepper
3 T. chopped olives	1 small clove garlic, minced
1 T. finely chopped parsley	1 large onion, grated
1/4 t. thyme	1/4 t. black pepper

1/2 pound grated cheese (mozzarella is best)

Roll biscuit dough to 1/8 inch and press into an oiled pan. Dot with butter and bake for 2 minutes in 450 degree oven. Mix together all ingredients except cheese and spread on crust. Layer cheese on top. Bake for 15 minutes at 350 degrees or until cooked and browned.

Moody Press, a ministry of Moody Bible Institute, is designed for education, evangelization, and edification. If we may assist you in knowing more about Christ and the Christian life, please write us without obligation: Moody Press, c/o MLM, Chicago, Illinois 60610.